a brit's guide

getting
married
abroad

getting married abroad

the complete guide to wedding packages

amanda statham

foulsham
LONDON • NEW YORK • TORONTO • SYDNEY

foulsham

The Publishing House, Bennetts Close, Cippenham,
Slough, Berkshire, SL1 5AP, England

ISBN 0-572-02920-9

Front cover photographs © Powerstock (top left);
Leonardo.com (bottom left); Bermuda Tourist
Authority (top and bottom right).

Back cover photographs © Ottley's Plantation Inn (left);
Powerstock (centre); Leonardo.com (right).

Photograph page 2: An idyllic wedding setting in Bermuda

While every effort has been made to ensure the accuracy of
all the information contained within this book, neither the
author nor the publisher can be liable for any errors. In
particular, since laws change from time to time and currency
rates change regularly, it is vital that each individual checks
relevant legal details for themselves.

Printed in Malaysia

CONTENTS

INTRODUCTION

Imagine exchanging vows in a hot-air balloon above Las Vegas or saying 'I will' in a chapel made of ice! These days there really is no limit as to where on earth, and above and below it, you can tie the knot. If you're tempted to fly off to exotic climes to marry, then you're not alone. One in three marriages between UK residents now takes place abroad, with a steady rise each year in the number of couples jetting off for guaranteed sunshine and a hassle-free, laid-back wedding.

The most popular choice of Brits abroad is still a beach wedding. Far-flung destinations such as the Caribbean, Maldives, Seychelles and Mauritius are all paradise islands that provide the perfect place to exchange vows. A white-sand beach at sunset is no longer the only foreign wedding choice however: with a little imagination and some good forward planning there is a huge array of destinations that are guaranteed to make your wedding the most memorable day of your life.

Get back to nature and arrive at your ceremony on an elephant in Sri Lanka; or take to the ocean with two dolphins and a minister to say 'I will' in Florida; reveal the depth of your love by marrying under water; or how about having the ceremony above the surface on board a boat in Sydney Harbour?

If you're put off by the idea of lots of red tape, don't be. This book is packed with helpful tips and hints on everything you need to know about marrying abroad.

It aims to ensure that you not only find the wedding destination of your dreams, but that you also arrange the whole occasion in the quickest, easiest way. So, whatever your concerns are – whether it's the documentation you need for a particular country, or how to get your wedding dress to your dream destination – we've got it covered.

A beautiful Bermuda chapel wedding

CHAPTER 1

PLANNING

The key to a great wedding abroad is to make sure that you are super-organised. As far as possible, you should try to sort out as much as you can before you leave. This will go a long way to ensuring that you don't meet with any nasty surprises once you arrive at your dream destination. Weddings abroad are much easier to plan nowadays because of modern aids like the internet, which gives you easy access to information about the country in which you want to marry, as well as the chance to see the actual hotels and other locations where you may want to tie the knot.

Before you do anything, there are a few questions you and your partner must ask yourselves. Do you both want to get married abroad? Do you agree on your dream destination? And, most important of all, can you marry there? (That's not as silly as it sounds – there are some places where a local marriage ceremony would not be recognised in the UK.)

Is a wedding abroad right for us?

Running off to marry in an exotic clime has got lots of appeal. You avoid the hassle of months of preparations that a UK wedding inevitably involves and it can all seem unbearably romantic – just the two of you declaring your undying love for each other as the sun sets over a sparkling ocean. However, you need to take some time out together to discuss whether this rosy picture really is right for you. Your first consideration is whether you both want to marry abroad. If one of you is keen but the other more reluctant, you need to chat about why this is so. Is it because of family commitments? Religious convictions? Anxiety about the unknown? Fear of flying?

If one of you really isn't keen on the idea, then you may be able to reach a compromise, such as having a ceremony in the UK, followed by a romantic blessing on your honeymoon. Or, if it's family commitments that are proving the problem, you could suggest that they all fly out to the destination to join in the fun.

Even if you're both keen to marry abroad, there are still some serious issues to think about before you take the plunge and start booking flights and arranging accommodation. The main complaint from brides about foreign weddings is lack of control. If you're the type of person who likes to plan everything, then you may not be happy to have arrangements for the biggest day of your life made halfway across the world without you there.

These days technological advances like e-mail and the internet help enormously, as you are able to keep in constant contact with wedding organisers and hotels. You can even send photographs of your perfect bouquet or wedding cake. However, that still can't guarantee that everything will be exactly as you anticipated it when you arrive. If you are not the sort of person who would see the funny side if things didn't go exactly according to plan, then it would be wise to hire a reputable wedding organiser with experience of weddings abroad who will tailor-make your big day from start to finish. Tour operators that specialise in weddings are also a good bet for those who want to know exactly what they are getting. Most have several wedding ceremony packages to choose from, which you can customise to suit yourself, by adding extras such as a video recording.

Then there is the issue of your families. A wedding abroad can be a smart move for couples who have family problems or who don't have any close family. However, if you do have relatives that you know would be upset by your decision to marry abroad, think carefully whether you'll regret the decision later on. Ultimately, where you exchange your vows is up to you, but it's important to consider their feelings too. If you do want to be surrounded by family on your big day, you'll have to consider the costs of flying everyone out to the destination. A wedding abroad is usually a cheaper option than a ceremony in the UK, but if you start inviting guests the price can soar. Also don't forget that there may be some relatives who may not want – or be able – to travel to your chosen location, such as elderly grandparents or those with very young children.

On the other hand, if you do invite your family and friends away with you to join in the celebrations,

a serious consideration has to be whether you want them with you on your honeymoon! Even if you stay in separate hotels or resorts, you're going to feel obliged to meet up with people before they fly home. Getting up for an early breakfast and then waving goodbye to your Auntie Hilda can break into your holiday and can take the romantic edge off your first day as man and wife in paradise!

Another potential problem is how you'll feel when the wedding is over. If you choose to have your wedding in the UK, you will probably have the first night to savour and the anticipation of flying off on honeymoon to keep you from feeling 'flat' after the excitement of the ceremony is over. If you're on a wedding and honeymoon combined, then you're already in paradise, so how do you top that? It's possible that you may feel you lose something of the magic if you're back on the beach in less than an hour.

Finally, don't underestimate the lure of the big white wedding. Most girls, deep down, have always wanted to walk up the aisle in a veil and white dress and there are a great many men out there who quite fancy the look of themselves in a full morning suit. If that's not you, then there will be no problem, but if you've always secretly rather liked the idea of a big English country wedding, then you should consider carefully whether a marriage abroad is for you. This will be, most likely, a once-in-a-lifetime experience, and you don't want to look back on your wedding day in 20 years' time and wish you had taken a more traditional approach.

If you need more help to decide whether a wedding abroad is for you, consult our handy wedding abroad pros and cons list below. It's simple: if you tick more of one category than the other, then that's the choice for your big day!

Where should we go?

Okay, you've weighed up the pros and cons and you've still got your heart set on marrying abroad. The next step is to start looking into where you want to go and to find out about how to marry there.

It can be quite daunting deciding on a destination for your summer holiday when you've got much of the world to choose from. Deciding the place where you're going to have your wedding day is even harder. It's best to start by thinking of exactly what sort of wedding you want and ruling out destinations that don't suit it.

You can halve the number of destinations available to you by simply deciding what sort of weather you want. For example, if you want a snow-covered winter wedding, then think about locations such as the Alps or Canadian Rockies, or even the Arctic Circle. If it's sun-kissed beaches, then go for the islands of the Caribbean, the Pacific or the Indian Ocean. It's important to remember, however, that while you can control the size of your wedding cake and what flowers to have in your bouquet, you can't control the weather. There are very few places in the world where you are absolutely guaranteed it won't rain (usually a desert!) You may have your heart set on a sunny beach wedding or the crisp, blue skies on top of a mountain, and make your

---

Getting married abroad – the pros and cons

Pros

- It's the hassle-free option to getting married, particularly if you book through a specialist tour operator.
- It's cheap! If you're on a budget and know that you can't afford the price of a British wedding (£14,000 on average), then it's a great option.
- You can invite as many or as few guests as you like, and uninvited people are less likely to be offended.

Cons

- You may feel a lack of control about arrangements and will only be able to see preparations once you are at the destination, which may be too late to make changes.
- You may feel flat once the ceremony is over.
- Your relatives and friends may be offended if they can't come.
- You may end up regretting not having family and friends there to celebrate with you.
- If they do come, you will have to share your honeymoon with them.

destination choice accordingly, but the weather may still let you down. However, you can reduce the odds of this happening by travelling to your destination at the optimum time of year for good weather.

This means that your decision on where you want to travel to will be strongly influenced by the time of year when you want to marry. The two have to be taken in tandem. For example, many of the destinations associated with sun and sand weddings, such as the Caribbean, actually have their best weather during the winter months of December to March and, although they do have hot temperatures all the year round, there is a definite hurricane season. You may not be so unlucky as to experience a full-blown tropical storm, but in most places there will be some rain on an almost daily basis. In the same way, the Seychelles and the Maldives in the Indian Ocean enjoy hot temperatures all the year round, but the chances of dry weather are also better during our winter, and you must take care to avoid the monsoon season. The entries for each of the destinations featured in this book include information about the climate and best times to travel there for dry weather. It's also a good idea to consult travel agents and tourist boards.

Long-haul or short-haul?

Weddings abroad always conjure up images of sunsets and palm-fringed beaches, but many couples are increasingly sticking closer to home to exchange vows. Short-haul destinations are becoming more and more popular, being ideal for time-pressed couples and easier for family and friends to reach. There are also some of the most romantic destinations in the world right on our doorstep – think of Paris, or the Amalfi Coast in Italy, or the idyllic little white chapels of Cyprus.

One disadvantage of short-haul destinations can be unreliable weather. Although, as I've just said, there is no place where you can be guaranteed sunshine, there is a far greater likelihood of consistently cloudless blue skies in a destination such as Hawaii than there is in the Dordogne.

Money is another factor: you may think that you're saving hard-earned cash by sticking close to home, but it can often work out more expensive as the costs of accommodation, food and beverages can mount up very quickly in European destinations. It's hard for our continental neighbours to compete with resorts such as Sandals in the Caribbean, which actually offer free wedding ceremonies as part of a seven-day honeymoon deal.

The Moulin Rouge in Paris

But the real downside of short-haul destinations available to UK couples is that they can be surprisingly complicated places to arrange weddings in. The time you will save by flying to Barcelona rather than Barbados may well be taken up with wading through the red tape and documentation provided by the Spanish authorities! For advice on which documents to take and how to apply for a licence in Europe, consult Chapter 3, starting on page 28.

Once you have chosen your destination, it is advisable to contact its embassy in your home country for advice on arranging your wedding. In the case of countries such as Italy and France, it is well worth employing the services of a company with experience of planning weddings for UK couples. If you decide to do it all yourself, it's advisable to start the process up to six months in advance to allow paperwork to be processed in good time.

Your wedding questionnaire

If you're really having difficulties making up your mind about your dream destination, the following questionnaire should help. You and your partner should fill it in separately and compare your answers. In each case, simply choose the answer that most suits you. At the end, tot up how many As, Bs, Cs or Ds you've scored and find out where you should be heading for your dream day.

So, pens at the ready … have fun!

What's your favourite kind of holiday?
A Relaxing in the sun
B Sightseeing
C A mix of relaxing and sightseeing
D Adventure and risk-taking activities

Which of these best describes how you choose a holiday?
A Return to the same place year after year
B Try new places but in the same area
C Go somewhere new each time
D Stick a pin in a map and head off

What type of holiday do you usually book?
A All-inclusive bargain deals
B Short breaks within your budget
C Luxurious, tailor-made holidays
D You don't book, you just go and find somewhere when you've landed

How do you like to relax?
A Watching TV
B Reading a book
C Going for a swim
D Sky-diving

What's your idea of travelling light?
A Two suitcases containing the entire contents of your wardrobe and bathroom
B One item of hand luggage
C A Louis Vuitton hold-all
D A passport and wallet

When do you normally holiday?
A One two-week break in the summer
B Lots of weekend breaks throughout the year

C Summer and winter trips away
D Wherever, whenever

How do you feel about flying?
A It's a necessary evil
B Short trips are fine
C You enjoy it, as long as you're upgraded
D Hot-air balloon or hang-glider – whatever!

How do you normally travel?
A Economy class
B Business class
C First class
D In the cockpit

How do boat trips make you feel?
A Sick
B Adventurous
C Glamorous
D Exhilarated

How do you spend your holiday time when abroad?
A Stay in your resort
B Do lots of sightseeing
C Venture out for meals and excursions
D Bond with the locals

What is your favourite type of weather?
A Hot, hot, hot
B Crisp, cool and clear
C Pleasantly warm and breezy
D Extreme

What can't you do without on holiday?
A Your suntan lotion
B Your guidebooks
C Your sunglasses
D Your rucksack

Mostly As
You're a sun-worshipper who likes nothing better than to spend two weeks lounging on a beach or by the pool, interrupted by nothing more than a quick trip to the bar or restaurant. Your idea of paradise is a white-sand, palm-fringed beach with nothing but blue skies and turquoise ocean for as far as the eye can see. You want to get married abroad because it's the hassle-free option and, if you book with the right tour operator, everything will be taken care of for you. Your ideal destination is the Indian Ocean or Caribbean, where you'll be able to enjoy a beachside ceremony in relaxed surroundings. Turn to Chapters 5 and 6 to find out more.

Mostly Bs
You're a culture vulture who isn't content to lie on a beach all day. You need much more to keep you occupied during your time away together, including good restaurants, bars and possibly some culture in the form of museums or art galleries.

You're not that bothered about the weather, as long as you have great landscapes and new experiences. You won't have to go far from the UK for your ideal wedding destination, but you're looking for hot and dry weather, so a romantic European destination in summertime will suit you perfectly (see Chapter 3). Either Italy or France would be an ideal destination for you, where you're guaranteed great food and fabulous scenery too.

Mostly Cs
You're an active type who likes to travel to far-flung destinations that offer more than just sun and sand.

You're also not worried about your budget. Whether you're zooming down a ski slope in the Rockies, lying on a yacht in the Bahamas or saying 'I will' in New York, you want to be somewhere a little unusual but not too far off the beaten track as you do enjoy life's little luxuries. You would benefit from employing a specialist wedding co-ordinator to customise your wedding day in an exotic location such as Africa or New Zealand. See Chapters 4 and 8 for lots of information. There are also destinations in the USA that would appeal, such as Los Angeles or Arizona (see Chapter 9).

Mostly Ds

You're an adrenalin junkie who wants a wedding day that no one will ever forget. You're likely to want to get hitched jumping out of a plane or whirling around on a theme park ride. You don't mind where it is as long as it's exciting and fun, and you'll remember it for ever. There are lots of ideas in this book (see Chapter 12), such as a hot-air balloon wedding in Africa, exchanging vows in a chapel made of ice, underwater weddings and ceremonies with dolphins.

Snows at Aspen, Colorado

Travel tip

If you're going abroad to get married, be sure to let every organisation you deal with know that it's for your wedding and you'll be amazed at how many free extras you'll receive.

- Tell the airline that you travel with that you're a wedding couple and you may get a free upgrade – just think of the leg room if you're shy about coming forward – and many airlines will also issue you with a complimentary glass of bubbly to start your 'weddingmoon' in style.

- Tell the hotel and you may be given a room upgrade. There are also likely to be gifts provided for honeymoon couples, such as a fruit basket, a bottle of sparkling wine or some special chocolates.

Booking your wedding

Once you've whittled your selection down to a few places, it's time to get down to the hard work of making your dream become a reality. When it comes to booking the event, there are several options open to you. You can do it through an ordinary tour operator, or a specialist wedding organiser, or you can do it yourself. One of the first ports of call should be your local travel agent, who will be able to guide you to appropriate travel brochures and, once you've chosen your destination, advise you about whether you're going to be able to arrange your wedding direct or through a tour operator.

Tour operators

Lots of tour operators, including Kuoni and Thomas Cook, offer a specialist wedding programme for popular destinations such as the Caribbean and the Maldives for very reasonable prices. These packages are ideal if you want it to be just the two of you or a small group (some offer group incentive discounts), and you're happy with just a few basic add-ons, such as bouquet, cake and champagne. Most of the ceremonies can be carried out either on the beach or a bower in hotel gardens. These really are the simplest option if you want a hassle-free wedding. Literally everything is taken care of for you, including flights, transfers, accommodation and all of the wedding details. However, what they can lack is uniqueness, that special individual touch.

The usual procedure when you book your wedding through the tour operator is that they will ask for a deposit (usually between £100 and £200), and then you and your partner must both fill in a form with your personal details. The tour operator will then request your preferred date at your destination. Bear in mind that many resorts have a maximum number of weddings a day, so it is wise to have a number of dates available.

The details of the package offered will vary from one operator to another, so it is important to establish before you book exactly what you are getting for your money. In particular, do make sure that you check legal status and insurance requirements.

Hotel Monasterio, Peru

Questions to ask your tour operator

- What exactly is included in the wedding package?
- Where will the ceremony take place?
- Does the hotel restrict the number of weddings that take place each day?
- What happens if it rains? Can the wedding be postponed for another day? Is there an alternative indoor venue?
- Does the hotel have an in-house wedding co-ordinator?
- Do they have an e-mail address? (This will give you easy communication through different time zones and also save on phone bills.)

Wedding specialists

If you're after something a little more individual – perhaps a venue off the beaten track – or you need to cater for a large party, it is worth tracking down a company abroad that specialises in organising weddings. They will be able to tailor-make your ceremony to your exact requirements (see Useful Addresses, page 186, for professionals in various countries). You'll also need an expert if you're planning to marry somewhere where it's harder for non-residents to organise, such as Italy.

Doing it yourself

It is quite possible to organise your own foreign ceremony, but before you begin, you must realise that you'll need to be meticulous in your planning of every detail, from the licence to the minister's fees. It is a huge help to have access to e-mail if you're going it alone, as it allows you to converse with foreign wedding co-ordinators and hoteliers on-line for just the cost of a local phone call. I would strongly recommend that you put everything in writing, and back up any correspondence with a final phone call before you set off, just to make sure that all your messages have been received and that your requests are in hand.

As well as making all the arrangements for the ceremony, you will have to book your own flights. When it comes to doing this, you must make sure that you will be in the country long enough to satisfy local residency requirements before the date of the wedding – many countries have a required temporary residency ruling, which may be only a few days, but possibly longer.

You'll also need to arrange transfers from your landing destination to your chosen hotel, and transport to the wedding ceremony if necessary.

Legal matters

Whoever makes the arrangements, it's important to check that the wedding you're planning is going to be valid in the UK – you don't want to end up like Jerry Hall who, having married Rolling Stone Mick Jagger in Bali, recently discovered that the marriage was never legally binding back in Britain!

Advice from the Foreign and Commonwealth Office in the UK states that it is important to consult the embassy or high commission in London of the country where you want to get married. This information will enable you to follow any necessary procedures you need to go through to make sure your wedding is legally recognised in the UK.

As a rule, if you marry under the local law of the country you've chosen and you have a marriage certificate issued, your wedding will be recognised as legal. It is worth noting that you can't register your marriage in the UK if you marry abroad. You can arrange for your marriage certificate to be deposited at the General Register office in the UK, but this isn't compulsory and it won't affect the validity of your marriage if you don't do it.

Guests

Weddings abroad are all very well if you want just the two of you to go jetting off into the sunset, but what if you're going to invite family and friends to your special occasion? This is an area that can cause real problems, so you should give it plenty of consideration before you start booking anything – it will only get complicated if you let it.

Deciding who to invite

Start by making a list of those guests you have to invite. This usually includes both sets of parents (or step-parents), siblings and one or two best friends. If you want to cut it to the absolute minimum, then you could just invite your parents. Nowadays, many couples take no one but their two best friends, to be best man and bridesmaid on the big day. This last arrangement requires some nerve, and also a great deal of tact when it comes to informing the family left behind!

There's no set etiquette for whom you must invite, but bear in mind that there are relatives who may be deeply offended if they're not included. It's important to consider how comfortable you will feel if that happens, and to be realistic about your particular family situation.

On the other hand, remember that your guests won't be able to leave after the ceremony, as they would in the UK – they will be together for days, possibly a week, if you've gone long-haul. How well do they all get on? Will they be exchanging addresses or blows by the end of the week?

Another important consideration is the fact that wherever you get married, without exception, you will need two witnesses to attend the ceremonies at destinations listed in this book, and indeed in most places around the world. Therefore, if you invite your two best pals, you've automatically got two witnesses, free of charge – and some hotels and resorts do actually charge you a small fee for providing witnesses!

Who pays for them?

This is another tricky area, so don't allow it to become a big issue. It may be that you are one of those lucky few who could afford to pay for the whole thing, including your guests' accommodation and air fares. But this is out of the question for most of us. If you simply don't have the budget to cover tickets for your close family and friends, then you have to make this clear from the word go. People will have to understand that you are planning your big day, and not their holiday. If they can't afford to come, then that's very sad but there's nothing you can do about it.

One option could be to split the costs – you could ask friends and family to pay for their fares, and in return you offer to pay for their accommodation. This is a particularly good idea if you're planning to take over a small hotel or guest house as you may get discounted rates. Alternatively, you could suggest that people don't buy you a wedding present and put the money toward the cost of their flight and hotel instead.

In some cases parents may offer a budget to help guests fly out, particularly if they had been expecting to pay for a wedding at home. It is quite likely that a small wedding abroad will cost as little as a third of a large white wedding in the UK!

Where will everyone stay?

A good tip is to house guests in a separate hotel or resort, some distance from the bridal couple. This means that they can have the fun of preparing for the wedding together (and discussing it afterwards!) while you can escape from any prying eyes.

Alternatively, some brides like their mother to be on hand on their wedding morning, so it may be advisable for her parents to stay in the same hotel as the couple, but other friends and family to stay elsewhere close by.

Do check whether you receive a discount for booking in a party. Many tour operators offer excellent reductions if you're travelling together and staying at the same venue, which is worth taking into account if you're on a tight budget.

You should check that your guests will be able to get to the place where you've chosen to tie the knot if they are staying elsewhere. If you're staying in a private resort, you may have to arrange entry passes for them. These are usually payable on a daily basis and will allow them access to all the facilities.

Romantic Bermuda

What about the ones left behind?
If you really feel you can't invite a big crowd, then there are still ways to make everyone feel involved. You could arrange for a blessing to be held on your return to the UK. It may only be symbolic, but you can invite lots of people to see you both exchange vows and congratulate you on your new marriage.

If you feel that you're letting down too many of your close friends, then you could suggest a really sensational stag or hen party to celebrate. There are lots of special packages on offer nowadays, including weekends abroad in venues such as Amsterdam or Prague. That way even though they've missed out on your wedding day, they will still have enjoyed the build-up to the celebrations.

One of the best ways to appease relatives and close friends is to organise a huge party on your return. This is a very popular choice for modern brides and grooms who have married abroad. It's a great idea to theme the party to suit the style of your wedding, so if you got married in Las Vegas, you could hire an Elvis impersonator, or if you married in Hawaii, greet your guests with garlands of flowers and serve up exotic cocktails. If you have had a video made of the wedding ceremony, you can play this on a large screen at the party, or get copies made of the original and hand them out to guests as they leave.

The budget
It's true that a wedding abroad generally costs a lot less than the average wedding in the UK, which is

now around £14,000. However, it's still most likely to be one of the most expensive trips of your life. There are lots of unexpected costs that creep into the arrangements, such as hairdressing and manicures, and of course you will want to go on excursions while you're there – and it all mounts up.

For this reason, it's worth starting to save up as soon as possible after your engagement just as you would for a traditional UK wedding. Even if you can only put aside a small amount every month, it's going to be a huge help when you come to make the full payment.

I have already said that you should give yourselves as long as possible to make sure that all of the arrangements are in place. This will also give you enough time to set aside a reserve of cash to pay for them.

When you start to plan your wedding, however long you have in advance, it is a good idea to write down an estimate of your costs. Include everything you can think of (see the checklist below), and then make sure you keep a record of exactly what is being spent and how. You will then be able to see if you are overspending – or saving money.

Finances checklist		
	Estimate	Actual cost
Transport and accommodation		
Flights (if separate)		
Hotel		
Transfers (if separate)		
Ceremony and reception		
Weddings rings		
Bride's outfit		
Groom's outfit		
Wedding cake		
Flowers		
Champagne		
Photography		
Video		
Music		
Minister's fee		
Licence		
Food		
Extras		
Excursions		
Meals		
Drinks		
Souvenirs		

If you are on a really tight budget, there are some resorts where weddings are conducted for free. They usually require you to stay for at least seven nights, and offer only a basic package of minister, flowers and cake. Look out for them throughout the book.

Another way to save money, or at least to stop spending it so heavily, is to tell everyone you talk to – the tour operator, the hotel, the airline – that you are organising your wedding and honeymoon! You want to get as many upgrades, bottles of champagne and extra services as you can, and saying you're about to be newlyweds is the best way to do it.

Style and beauty

You may have your destination all set, but the other big decision is what do you wear on the big day?

Wedding outfits

Important considerations if you're wearing traditional outfits are what time of day you're getting married and what the temperatures will be. It's not advisable to marry in very hot temperatures in tight, restricting clothing as you'll only end up looking hot and sweaty in your photographs. If you do want to wear the full traditional outfits and you're getting married somewhere tropical, ask to have your wedding booked at a time when temperatures are cooler, such as sunrise or sunset.

In warm climates, it's more advisable to wear lightweight loose clothing that will allow you to stay cool and look the part! You can always brighten up your outfit with tropical flowers. If you want to wear

something more daring such as a bikini, check beforehand with the officiating minister to make sure this is acceptable – some countries will insist that your shoulders and chest be covered for the ceremony.

It's important to be practical when you're looking for your wedding outfit in terms of your specific ceremony. If you're marrying in the basket of a hot-air balloon, is there going to be room for the groom and the minister if the bride is wearing a billowing wedding dress? If you're exchanging vows on a snow-covered mountain slope, you're going to need to be protected against the cold.

If you've got your heart set on a full-skirted white wedding gown for the bride and a full morning suit for the groom despite the fact that you're marrying abroad, then remember to tell staff on the airline, or whatever form of transport you're travelling in, to stow them away carefully. It is best to get them boxed up professionally and then hang them up as soon as you reach your hotel destination. If it's possible, they should be steam ironed (if you can't arrange this, hang your outfits in a steam-filled bathroom, to help the creases drop out).

The bride's hair and make-up

If you're getting married at a private holiday resort, then you'll find that most of them have a beauty salon where you can make an appointment to get prepared for the big day – although check to see what services they offer beforehand. If you're doing your own hair, keep it simple. A flower tucked behind

your ear can look just as good as a
tiara! The best way to make sure that
your hair doesn't go dry and brittle
or change colour in the sun is to
wear a hat for the days preceding the
ceremony. If you do have to expose
your hair to the sun, make sure that
you buy a sunscreen for your hair
that contains a UV filter. You can
also buy after-sun products for your
hair that will condition it and
redress any damage caused by salt
water and heat. If your hair tends to
go frizzy in the heat, invest in a
serum that will make it sleek and
shiny no matter how hot and humid
the weather is.

If you've chosen a hot
destination and you've been in the
country for several days before you
can get married, you may well have
acquired a tan (take care not to get
'strap marks' if your dress is low-cut).
If you're going to wear foundation
on your wedding day, it's advisable
to choose a shade several shades
darker than your normal one. Better
still, use a tinted moisturiser that
allows you natural glow to shine
through. It is probably best to keep
your make-up to a minimum – you
certainly won't need the full
treatment that you might have opted
for at home. A sweep of mascara and
a dab of lip gloss may be all you
need, but don't forget to pack a
bronzer and brush to sweep over
your cheeks, forehead and nose for
that lovely sun-kissed look.

What to pack

Before you start to pack, make a list.
This is one occasion when you really
can't afford to leave something
essential behind.

Top of your list will be your
wedding outfits. If you are flying,
these will almost certainly be too
large to be carried on to the aircraft
as hand baggage – unless you are
travelling first class. They will have
to go in a suitcase with the rest of
your belongings. You will also need
casual daywear, including trainers,
sandals and swimwear, and probably
some smarter clothes for the
evening. Don't forget plenty of
nightwear (if you use it!) and
underwear, including any special
items for the wedding day. Make a
full list of the toiletries you will
need, including sunscreen,
mosquito repellent and all the
bride's cosmetics. Most of these can
be packed in your suitcase, but do
take care to wrap anything that may
leak in a plastic bag. You don't want
to end up with after-sun moisturiser
all over the groom's shirt.

Valuable items, such as jewellery
and money, are best carried in your
hand luggage. You will also need to
have your passport to hand. You can
carry your camera, portable CD
player and any reading materials
with you, as well as a small quantity
of toiletries. Always take essential
medication with you in your hand
luggage. Never pack it in your
suitcase – it may not arrive at your
destination at the same time as you.
If you are a diabetic and need to
carry hypodermic needles with you,
check with the airline beforehand, as
they may wish to remove them from
you for security reasons.

Health advice

If you are planning to go to a long-
haul destination, you should both

visit your doctor well in advance – at least eight weeks before departure – to find out what medication or injections you need to protect you during your stay. Inoculation requirements vary from country to country, so even if you've had some jabs recently, do get up-to-date advice from your doctor or practice nurse on what you will require. Wherever you are going, even if it's only to Europe, it's a good idea to make sure that your tetanus jabs are up to date.

If you are going to a country that is affected by malaria, you would be wise to take anti-malaria tablets. These need to be taken for some time before you go, and should be continued after you return to the UK. They may have had some bad press recently, but the disease is very serious – the world's biggest killer, in fact – so it's still better to take them if you're at risk particularly as the latest tablets have far fewer side effects.

Your local medical practice will have full information on the protection you will need for the area you are going to visit. You can also find lots of useful information on the net on www.fitfortravel.scot.nhs.uk/.

For brides who are on the pill, unless you want to conceive during your honeymoon, it's wise to take a pack of condoms with you. If you catch any kind of tummy bug, this can make the pill less effective and expose you to the risk of pregnancy. If you don't want your period to occur while you're away, it is possible to continue taking the pill without a break between packets to keep it at bay, but consult your GP first before you decide to do this.

Documentation

You will have to take some documents with you from the UK, including your passport – of course – and, usually, your birth certificate.

Uluru (Ayers Rock), Australia

El Kelaa, Morocco

You may be required to produce other documents to prove certain facts before you are legally able to marry. Some of these must be prepared before you leave home.

You may need to produce an affidavit, or certificate of no impediment, which lists detailed information about your marital status, to confirm that you're single and free to marry. It can be obtained from a notary. To find one, look in your telephone directory or ask at any solicitor's office. Costs vary from solicitor to solicitor, and the solicitor's office will need to stamp and sign the affidavit.

If either of you is widowed, you must provide the original of your previous marriage certificate to show that you were legally married, and the death certificate of your previous spouse to show that they are now deceased.

If either of you is divorced, or your marriage has been annulled, evidence has to be provided in most countries to show that the marriage is legally ended. You may need to produce your certificate of decree absolute, which bears a red embossed court seal. If you don't have the original, an additional copy can be obtained by application to the court that handled the divorce, quoting the full names of the divorced parties and court matter number.

In many countries you will be expected to produce your birth certificates in order to confirm your date of birth.

If either of you is adopted, you may have to produce adoption papers as evidence.

Providing certified documents

If you do not have the original documents, or do not wish to carry them with you, it is possible to arrange for original documents, such as birth certificates, to be copied. Ordinary photocopies will not be accepted. You need a solicitor to carry out the process who has been legally authorised to do it. Every copy must be stamped and signed to indicate that it is a true copy of the original. It's best to ensure that signatures are made in a coloured ink, such as red or blue, rather than black, so that authorities in your chosen country know that it is a certified copy rather than just a photocopy.

Wedding day countdown!

Whether you're arranging your own wedding or leaving it in the capable hands of a specialist or travel agent, there are still things that you're going to have to remember to do for this one-in-a-life-time trip. Use this helpful six-month countdown to make sure you stay on top and don't forget anything!

Six months to go...
- Choose where you want to go for your wedding abroad.
- Check how many days you'll need to be there before you can marry and all the legal requirements.
- Decide how many guests you will have – if any.
- Armed with this information, book the flights, venue and accommodation.

Three months to go...
- Check that you have all of the documents that you'll need, such as valid 10-year passports and birth certificates. If not, apply now.
- Confirm your guest list with your travel agent/co-ordinator/hotel.
- Choose outfits.
- Check with your GP to see if you need any inoculations for your destination.
- Choose wedding rings.
- Arrange reception details, such as flowers, cake, etc.
- Book hair/make-up appointments at your destination for the day of wedding (if possible).

One month to go...
- Check that you have all original documents ready.
- Make sure you have suitable luggage to transport your wedding outfits.
- Buy foreign currency.

One week to go...
- Check flight details and confirm if necessary.
- Arrange transport or overnight accommodation at airport if necessary.

The day before...
- You're now at your destination, so check that everything is as planned.
- Meet with the wedding co-ordinator at the venue and confirm all the reception arrangements.
- Meet the minister/registrar and arrange a quick run-through of the ceremony, if possible.
- Book a meal at a romantic restaurant to get in the mood!

On the day...
- Relax and enjoy it!

HOW TO USE THIS BOOK

First, look up your chosen destination in the Contents listing on pages 5–6, then turn to the appropriate section of the book. You will find a short description of each destination, followed by a series of entries, covering everything you need to know about planning your trip, what you need to take, how to get there and what to expect when you arrive.

Note that this book is intended as a guide only. Legal requirements may change at any time, so it is essential to consult the relevant embassy immediately before you travel to your chosen destination. The entries are headed as follows:

Travel time

This indicates roughly how long it will take you to get to the destination from the airport in the UK. Times will vary depending on whether there are stops en route and how often you need to change planes. Remember that, especially in more remote destinations, onward transfers may involve lengthy waits. The exact duration of flights will vary from one airline to another, as will the aircraft type. I have included details of onward connections by boat or small aircraft, where appropriate, but not the time taken to transfer from your final arrival point to your hotel.

Waiting period

This indicates how long you have to be in the country before you can get married. Some countries require a period of residency, others simply need time to process documents before a marriage licence can be handed out. Never underestimate this – the wheels of bureaucracy can grind very slowly indeed and you would be wise to allow a little extra time if possible.

Documents

This is a list of all the documents you will need to be able to marry in that country. Most countries need a form of ID, for which a valid 10-year passport will be acceptable. It is vital that you take **all** of the required listed documents with you, or send them off prior to the trip, otherwise you may find that you are unable to go ahead with the wedding.

Note: It is advisable to always bring the **originals** of your documents, such as birth certificates, unless otherwise stated. In many countries, photocopies aren't accepted, and you don't want to be caught out. Certified copies, as described on page 24, are usually – but not always – acceptable.

Be sure to check all documents very thoroughly before you leave the UK. Mistakes such as incorrect spelling may lead to the cancellation of your wedding.

Minimum age

This is the minimum age at which you can legally marry in that country without parental consent. In most countries, including the UK, you can marry if you are younger than this – usually 16 years

– with parental consent, but you always require written proof of this.

Further information

This section gives you lots of information on what to expect when you arrive at your destination. It will help you through the process of applying for your marriage licence, which in some countries is quite complicated. It also gives hints and tips about local regulations on where weddings can be performed and by whom.

Weather

This gives details of the best times to visit each country, indicating the dry and rainy periods, if appropriate. I have included average temperatures, so that you can plan your wedding outfit and pack appropriate clothing for the whole of your stay.

Contact details

This section gives telephone numbers, addresses and websites of local organisations, such as the local tourist board, consulate and embassy, that can provide information to help you to plan your perfect wedding abroad. In addition, for general information, I would recommend that you look at the numerous wedding-based websites on the net, such as: www.weddingguide.co.uk, www.barefootluxury.com, www.weddings.co.uk.

Dream hotels

Self-explanatory, really – this section describes some of the most fabulous, romantic hotels in each country, including full details of how to contact them direct. The vast majority of the dream hotels featured can arrange wedding ceremonies, the exceptions being in countries where couples must marry at a register office or where otherwise stated. The hotels are not cheap – but I make no apology for including them. If you want a once-in-a-lifetime experience to remember together for the rest of your days, this is where to find it.

Opposite: Riomaggiore, Italy

Peter Island Resort, British Virgin Islands

CHAPTER 3

EUROPE

Europe makes an ideal wedding destination if you don't want to travel long-haul to exchange your vows, but still want somewhere a little more special than just staying in the UK. One benefit of sticking closer to home is the fact that it's much easier for family and friends to join you for the big day. Europe's other allure is that it has some of the most wonderful wedding destinations in the world, and there is a wealth of snowy winter wonderlands and sun-baked picturesque Mediterranean villages, not to mention pretty white chapels, to choose from. The only problem you may encounter in some areas of Europe is that getting the marriage licence can be a complicated and lengthy process. If you've set your heart on marrying in a country where there's a lot of red tape, such as Italy or Spain, it's well worth enlisting the help of a specialist tour operator (see page 186).

HEALTH TIPS

- Another big advantage of travelling to Europe is that you won't need to have any injections!
- Do watch out for the water, though. In some places, particularly on more remote islands in the southern Mediterranean the water that comes out of the taps in your room may not be fit to drink so, if you don't want a tummy bug to spoil your honeymoon, stick to the bottled variety.

AUSTRIA

What could be more romantic than this land of soaring snowy mountains, deep forests, alpine meadows, sparkling lakes and fairy-tale castles, where you can taste both the invigorating mountain air and the baroque culture of elegant cities like Vienna and Salzburg – a paradise for classical music-lovers. If you love winter sports, there are superb skiing destinations to choose from and great snow conditions right through from November to April. So, winter or summer, spring or autumn, Austria is always enchantingly beautiful and has always made a special setting for a wedding day.

Travel time

Around 2 hours to Vienna.

Waiting period

None specified.

Documents

- Valid 10-year passports.
- Birth certificates.
- Certificate of no impediment, which must be obtained from your local register office not more than 6 months before your wedding date.
- Decree absolute (if divorced), marriage certificate and previous spouse's death certificate (if widowed), deed poll proof (if name changed).

Minimum age

19 years without parental consent. If either of you is under 19, you will need proof of parental consent in the form of a sworn affidavit.

Further information

You apply for the marriage licence at the *Standesamt* (register office) of the first district of Vienna (see Contact details). You must both attend in person taking all necessary documents with you. Originals or certified copies of documents must be sent to the register office where the marriage is to take place at least eight weeks prior to your intended date of marriage. Any affidavits and your certificate of no impediment must be translated into German. The embassy (see Contact details) will be able to help you find a translator. Austrian law only recognises civil marriages. However, if you have your heart set on a religious ceremony it is possible to have one after a civil ceremony has been solemnised. Civil marriages are performed by officials of the Vital Statistics Office and it is usual to hold them in a local register office.

 DREAM HOTEL

Hotel Sacher Salzburg

Schwarzstrasse 5–7, A–5020 Salzburg, Austria

Tel: 00 43 622 88977

E-mail: salzburg@sacher.com

Web: http://salzburg.sacher.com

The city of Salzburg's grandest, and most romantic, hotel. It lies on the quiet Salzach promenade and has been a favourite of actors, poets and politicians since the 1800s. Inside, couples will love the luxurious, airy rooms filled with antiques, chandeliers and elegant furnishings. In the summer, meals are served on the restaurant terrace, and the gourmet restaurant and piano bar are also very pleasant.

It is occasionally possible to arrange to have a civil ceremony somewhere other than a register office, such as on a mountainside, but as this is at the discretion of the individual registrar it's wise to ask in advance.

Weather

Cold from December to March with temperatures frequently below zero. Snow can be expected in the mountains from November to April – the higher the location, the more likely it is. Spring and summer months are ideal times to visit – temperatures can get as high as 32°C (90°F) from June to September.

Mountains near Mayrhofen, Austria

DREAM HOTEL
Grand Hotel Wien
Kärntner Ring 9, A–1010 Vienna, Austria
Tel: 00 43 1 515800
E-mail: reservation@grandhotelwien.com
Web: www.lhw.com/grandwien

A member of the Leading Hotels of the World group and located in the heart of one of Austria's most romantic cities, this hotel is an ideal spot for couples in love. It's close to the famous opera house and has a stunning French restaurant with a terrace overlooking the city – the perfect place to celebrate your marriage.

Contact details

Austrian Embassy
18 Belgrave Mews West, London SW1X 8HU
Tel: 020 7235 3731
Fax: 020 7344 0292
E-mail: embassy@austria.org.uk
Web: www.austria.org.uk

Austrian National Tourist Office
14 Cork Street, London W1X 1PF
Tel: 020 7629 0461
Fax: 020 7499 6038
E-mail: info@into.co.uk
Web: www.austria-tourism.at

Standesamt
Schlesingerplatz 3–6, 1080 Vienna, Austria
Tel: 00 43 140 134 0859
E-mail: post-a08@m61.magwein.gv.at
Web: www.wien.gv.at/ma61/sta.htm

CYPRUS

Where better to exchange your vows than the East Mediterranean island associated with Aphrodite, Greek goddess of love and beauty? Cyprus is only a short flight from the UK, so it's ideal if you're looking for a relaxing wedding destination with sun and sand but don't have the time to go long-haul. The other attraction of Cyprus is the sheer diversity of things to see and do: if you choose the right time of year, it's possible to ski in the mountains in the morning and spend the afternoon on the beach! There are also the historical towns of Limassol and Nicosia to discover and the rugged coastlines to explore.

Travel time
Around 4 hours 30 minutes.

Waiting period
3 full working days for a town hall ceremony; 5 for a church wedding.

Documents
- Valid 10-year passports.
- Birth certificates.
- Decree absolute (if divorced), marriage certificate and previous spouse's death certificate (if widowed), adoption certificate (if adopted), deed poll proof (if name changed).

- A single statutory declaration stating that both partners are free to marry and are single, divorced or widowed. It has to be signed and stamped by a solicitor and should state 'solicitor' on the document. The document must also show full name, address, religion, passport number and occupation for each of you. It has to be issued within three months of the proposed marriage date and must include your intent to marry in your chosen destination.

DREAM HOTEL
Annabelle

Poseidon Avenue, Paphos 8125, Cyprus
Tel: 00 357 0 26938 33
Web: www.thanoshotels.com

The Annabelle is an exclusive five-star hotel of unforgettable luxury and elegant charm. The landscaped gardens make an ideal location for a blessing, or staff can help you arrange a wedding in one of the nearby chapels. All of the 218 rooms, suites and garden suites are beautifully decorated and have lots of great touches like a well-stocked mini bar, fluffy bathrobes and private balconies or terraces offering uninterrupted views of the Mediterranean and the old fishing harbour of Paphos.

Petra tou Romious, Cyprus, birthplace of Aphrodite

DREAM HOTEL
Columbia Beach Hotel
PO Box 54042, 3779 Limassol, Cyprus
Tel: 00 357 25 22 12 01
E-mail: columbia@cytanet.com.cy
Web: www.columbia-hotels.com

Cyprus's best-kept secret is this luxury hotel, designed in the style of a Cypriot village, which occupies a prime location overlooking sweeping Pissouri Bay. It's an intimate and stylish retreat offering an ideal balance between leisure and activity, with an excellent range of land and sea sports. Both Paphos and Limassol are 30 minutes' drive away. There are two swimming pools, a jacuzzi and spa, and most of the bedrooms have panoramic views over the sandy bay. It also has a little chapel in the grounds where you can hold your wedding ceremony.

Minimum age
18 years without parental consent. If either of you is under 18, proof of parental consent is required in the form of an affidavit signed by a notary.

Further information
Once you have arrived in Cyprus, you need to complete application papers and sign a declaration of oath, after which you can obtain the marriage licence from the town hall, at a cost of around £200.

For Roman Catholic ceremonies, you must both provide certificates of baptism. For an Anglican ceremony, one or other of you must provide a certificate of baptism and must be able to give the name and address of the local vicar, parish priest or minister from your parish.

Weather
Lots of sunshine throughout the year with temperatures rising well over 32°C (90°F) from July to September. Winters are cooler and although most days are bright it can be miserably wet, particularly in January.

Contact details
Cyprus Tourist Office
17 Hanover Street, London W1R OAA
Tel: 020 7569 8800
E-mail: ctolon@ctolon.demon.co.uk
Web: www.visitcyprus.org.cy

DREAM HOTEL
Anassa
PO Box 66006, 8830 Polis, Cyprus
Tel: 00 357 26 888000
E-mail: res.anassa@thanoshotels.com
Web: www.thanoshotels.com

An enchanting blend of five-star luxury, classical architecture and complete privacy, Anassa looks across one of the finest beaches in Cyprus to the Akamas Peninsula and the famous baths of Aphrodite. All rooms are extraordinarily spacious, luxuriously furnished and have balconies with panoramic sea views, while some suites have private plunge pools and whirlpools on sea-facing terraces. There's also a Thalassa Spa specialising in the very latest health and beauty treatments. Newlyweds will love the Adonis and Aphrodite suites situated on the top floor of the resort, each having one bedroom with luxurious bathroom facilities and a whirlpool on the balcony. There's a beautiful church on the property and a wedding co-ordinator on hand to help you plan your big day to the last detail.

FRANCE

Paris, France's capital, is one of the most romantic cities in the world and it's only an hour away! But it's not only the stunning architecture, buzzy restaurants and swish hotels of Paris that tempt couples to marry in France, it's also the slopes of the Alps, the glorious cosmopolitan coastal destinations such as Biarritz, St Tropez and Nice and the beautiful countryside of the Dordogne and Loire valleys.

Travel time

Around 1 hour to Paris, 1 hour 45 mins to Lyon, 2 hours to Nice.

Waiting period

1 month.

 DREAM HOTEL
**Four Seasons George V
Paris**
31 Avenue George V, Paris, France 75008
Tel: 00 33 1 49 52 7000
Web: www.fourseasons.com

This city hotel is the perfect place for romantics. It's just a few steps from the Champs Elysées and boasts private terraces with views that span the whole of Paris. Seventeenth-century tapestries adorn its walls, its cuisine is world famous and the rooms are vast and yet comfortable. Best of all, you can get married here, with wedding co-ordinators on hand to make sure that everything runs smoothly. There are lots of different function rooms to choose from, and one of the world's most luxurious honeymoon suites for your first night – it's got five balconies with stunning views of the Eiffel Tower, a huge bed and a bathroom where you can stare out above the city from the tub. Pure heaven.

Documents

- Valid 10-year passports.
- Birth certificates with mother's and father's names, plus a French translation.
- Decree absolute (if divorced), marriage certificate and previous spouse's death certificate (if widowed).
- A prenuptial medical certificate – obtainable either from a GP in France, from the French Dispensary in London (020 7388 3215) or from the Medicare Centre in London (020 7370 4999).

Details of official translators are available from the French Consulate (see Contact details). Send a stamped, self-addressed envelope with your request.

Minimum age

18 for a man, 15 for a woman, without parental consent.

Further information

French authorities recommend employing the assistance of a specialist wedding agency (see Contact details) to help you make arrangements as it can be a fairly complicated process. Alternatively, you can arrange a wedding through selected hotels.

If you want a religious ceremony, you have to negotiate directly with the church where you wish to hold it, such as the American Church in Paris where tourists are able to marry (see Contact details). If you wish to have a civil ceremony in France, you must get in touch directly with the mayor's office of the town in which you wish to marry. By law, all French nationals have to have a civil

ceremony, which may then be
followed by a religious wedding.

Weather

Northern France has a climate
similar to the UK, but it gets much
warmer as you go south.
Temperatures on the Mediterranean
coast average 28°C (82°F) June to
August and a pleasant 21°C (70°F)
in the autumn.

Contact details

Maison de la France
(French Tourist Board)
178 Piccadilly, London W1J 9AL
Tel: 09068 244 123 (all calls 60p/min)
E-mail: info.uk@franceguide.com
Web: www.franceguide.com

French Consulate
6a Cromwell Place, London SW7 2EW
Web: www.ambafrance.org.uk

Four Seasons Hotel, Paris

DREAM HOTEL
**Château du Domanie
Saint-Martin**
Route de Coursegoules, 06140 Vence,
France
Tel: 00 33 493 580202
Web: www.chateâu-st-martin.com

This Relais and Châteaux hotel,
which is hidden away in 32 acres
of parkland just a few miles inland
from the French Riviera, is such a
treasure, you won't want anyone else
to know about it. It's incredibly
tranquil and the decor is superb.
Inside the main château are antiques,
original artworks, fresh flowers every
where and plush rugs that you sink
into. There are also guest villas
dotted around the grounds, each
with a bedroom, lounge and its own
private terrace with views of the
Mediterranean. The food there is
exceptionally good and there's a
pool to laze around in the summer.
Weddings can be arranged on an
individual basis.

American Church
65 Quai d'Orsay, 75007 Paris
Tel: 00 33 140 620500
Web: www.americanchurchparis.org

Wedding organisers

Association 'Oui' France
11 Rue Saint Florentin, 75008 Paris
Tel: 00 33 140 204090
Web: www.thematour.com

Just Married
10 Place Vendôme, 75001 Paris
Tel: 00 33 608 282034
Web: www.golden-star-events.com

France Information Line
09068 244123 (all calls 60p/min)

GERMANY

This is a large country with a huge variety of possible venues to consider. It's an attractive option if you're looking for somewhere quick and easy to get to, and where you're guaranteed great hotels, food and service. All of its major cities, such as Berlin, have a wealth of vibrant cultures and nightlife to discover, while a trip into Germany's countryside will reveal pretty valleys and snaking rivers.

Travel time

1–2 hours.

Waiting period

None specified.

Documents

- Valid 10-year passports.
- Birth certificates, which must give both your parents' names and be translated into German by a court-recognised translator.
- Decrees nisi and absolute (if divorced), marriage certificate and previous spouse's death certificate (if widowed).

DREAM HOTEL
Schlosshotel Kronberg

Hainstrasse 25, 61476 Kronberg, Germany
Tel: 00 49 0 6173 701 01
E-mail: info@schlosshotel-kronberg.de
Web: www.schlosshotel-kronberg.de

The former stately home of an Empress, this fairy-tale manor sits in the middle of a large park and is surrounded by manicured lawns and beautiful gardens. It's an exceptional place to have your wedding, and you can follow the civil ceremony with a reception in the library, the hotel lobby or in the park. It's considered one of Germany's finest hotels for good reason – it's bursting with character, from the antiques to the original artworks on the walls and the ornate dining room.

- A certificate of no impediment confirming you're eligible to marry, which has to be translated into German and legalised and stamped by a German embassy or consulate in the UK/Germany with an official stamp.

Neuschwanstein Castle, Germany

- A certificate of free status (*Ehenhigkeitszeugnis*) is required of all foreigners marrying in Germany – you can obtain this from your local register office in the UK.

Note: All documents submitted have to be translated into German (contact the German Embassy for details of approved translators). The processing, in most cases, will require up to a month, so allow yourself plenty of time.

Minimum age
18 years without parental consent. If either of you is under 18, you must have the written, notarised consent of both your parents or legal guardian.

Further information
Your registrar in Germany will send the documents you have provided to the *Oberlandesgericht* (regional court), who will then give you permission to marry. A fee, usually relevant to your monthly salary, is levied for the service, which may be doubled if you are divorced and the decree has to be studied. When you finally get the go-ahead, the civil ceremony may be performed at any register office *(Standesamt)*.

Note: A marriage in Germany is only recognised as legal if performed at a register office. However, an additional church ceremony may be held later, if desired.

Weather
Can be very cold and snowy in the winter months, particularly in eastern Germany with temperatures averaging 2°C (35°F) December to February. Summer months from July to August are generally warm and pleasant, about 24°C (75°F).

Contact details
German National Tourist Office
PO Box 2695, London W1A 3TN
Tel: 020 7317 0908
Web: www.germany-tourism.de

German Embassy
23 Belgrave Square, London SW1X 8PZ
Tel: 020 7824 1300
E-mail: mail@german-embassy.org.uk
Web: www.german-embassy.org.uk

 DREAM HOTEL
Park Hotel Bremen
Im Bürgerpark, 28209 Bremen, Germany
Tel: 00 49 421 34080
Web: www.lhw.com/parkbremen.de

This beautiful property has a country house atmosphere and is a member of the Leading Hotels of the World group. It's an ideal place for wedding celebrations, large or small, as there are seven elegant salons of various sizes for party gatherings. It's also a picturesque place to spend the first night of your honeymoon. Set in acres of wooded grounds and overlooking a stunning lake, the hotel offers plenty to see and do. Horse riding, thalassotherapy, Turkish baths, a heated outdoor pool and bike riding are just some of the things on offer. It's also renowned for its fine dining: there's the Park Restaurant for gourmet cuisine, La Fontana for international dishes and the Park Hotel Bar for letting your hair down and dancing!

GREECE AND THE GREEK ISLANDS

Greece makes a wonderful setting for a wedding, with an apparently limitless selection of magical settings and scenic backdrops for your big day. Culture vultures will adore the ancient ruins and history of the islands, sun-worshippers will love the climate and beaches while couples who want nightlife as well as a great landscape have lots of bustling towns to choose from. The only problem you'll have is choosing which island to settle on for your marriage ceremony. Crete is the largest and most well known, while Corfu and Rhodes are also popular with British couples.

Travel time

About 3 hours 30 minutes to Athens or Thessaloniki, 4 hours to Crete.

Waiting period

7 full working days on average – but it varies from one part of the country to another.

Documents

- Valid 10-year passports.
- Birth certificates.
- Certificate of no impediment, valid for 3 months.
- Decree absolute (if divorced), marriage certificate and previous spouse's death certificate (if widowed), adoption certificate (if adopted), deed poll proof (if name changed).

Minimum age

18 years without parental consent. If either of you is under 18, parental consent is needed in the form of a statutory declaration, stamped and signed by a solicitor.

Further information

The certificate of no impediment, together with birth certificates and all other relevant documents, should be sent to the Foreign Office to be legalised. This takes around ten days and costs approximately £12 per document. It's payable by cheque or postal office, made payable to the Foreign and Commonwealth Office (see Contact details). Once the documents have been legalised, you must send them to one of two independent translators approved by the Greek Embassy (see Contact details) who will translate the documents and arrange to have them stamped by the Embassy – it costs around £30 per translation and £13 per

 DREAM HOTEL
Elounda Beach Hotel and Villas
72053 Elounda, Crete, Greece
Tel: 00 30 28410 41412
E-mail: elohotel@eloundabeach.gr
Web: www.lhw.com/elounda

A member of the Leading Hotels of the World group, this lovely retreat has a small chapel in its grounds, which makes it an ideal destination if you want a hassle-free wedding in picturesque surroundings. The hotel is a gem, set in the north-east of Crete on Mirabello Bay, which certainly deserves its five stars. The accommodation rivals the best in Greece: villas have jacuzzis and steam baths, exclusive suites have a private heated swimming pool, while royal suites have indoor and outdoor pools, private butler, pianist and gym with trainer!

document. Payment may be made in cash, or by postal order or bankers draft. Cheques are not acceptable.

Once you are in Greece, you need to complete final documentation and marriage licence applications. In some areas, you are required to place an advertisement in the local paper giving notice of intent to marry. This costs around £60 and is payable locally.

Ceremonies are short and informal and are conducted in Greek, with a translator provided. The Greek tradition is to hold wedding ceremonies late in the day, as it's cooler. Civil ceremonies take place in the town hall, usually in the second week of a holiday, with the exception of the island of Zante where weddings can take place in less than seven days. If you want your wedding in a chapel, consider a hotel that has one on its premises.

Weather
Warm throughout the year, with July to August averaging 26°C (80°F).

Santorini, Greek Islands

DREAM HOTEL
Grand Resort Lagonissi
Sounio Avenue, 19010 Lagonissi, Athens, Greece
Tel: 00 30 22910 76000
E-mail: lagonissi@lagonissiresort.gr
Web: www.lagonissiresort.gr

This waterfront peninsula resort has a small chapel situated on a pretty hill in its grounds, which is a stunning location for weddings or renewals of vows. The hotel boasts luxury rooms with magnificent sea views as well as sea-front bungalows with private pools or private gardens. There are – count them! – 17 beaches, and the bedrooms are the last word in comfort. Other attractions include five restaurants in gardens or on the seashore offering a variety of cuisines, 24-hour butler service and meandering pathways through the lush gardens for romantic evening strolls. There's also an extensive water sports centre, an outdoor seawater swimming pool, floodlit tennis courts and a mini golf course.

Winter can be wet, particularly in the north and west, where temperatures drop to around 13°C (54°F) and don't really start to rise until the end of April.

Contact details
Greek/Hellenic Tourism Organisation
4 Conduit Street, London W1R ODJ
Tel: 020 7734 5997
Web: www.gnto.gr

Foreign and Commonwealth Office
The Legalisation Office, Old Admiralty Building, Whitehall, London SW1A 2LG
Tel: 020 7008 1111
Web: www.fco.gov.uk

ITALY

One of the world's most romantic countries, Italy has something for every couple looking for their ideal wedding location, from the rugged Alps and tranquil lakes in the north, to the cultural centres of Venice, Florence and Rome, down to the golden beaches in the south. However, be warned, getting married here can be a complicated process so you may want to employ the help of a professional! Despite this, it's a very popular honeymoon destination for Brits, being only a short flight away but offering the kind of standard of food, wine, accommodation and weather that you'd fly halfway across the world for.

Travel time

2–3 hours, depending on whether you are flying to the north or south.

Waiting period

Variable. Some register offices in Italy will require you to sign a declaration of intention to marry 2 to 4 days prior to your marriage ceremony, so you should check with the individual registrar.

Documents

- Valid 10-year passports.
- Birth certificates.
- Certificate of no impediment (see below).
- Previous spouse's death certificate (if widowed). Decree absolute (if divorced).

Note: In Italy, a divorced woman cannot remarry until 300 days after the dissolution of her previous marriage.

Minimum age

18 years without parental consent. If either of you is under 18, proof of parental consent is required, in the form of a sworn affidavit.

Further information

The certificate of no impediment must be obtained from your local register office. This will take around 21 days, and costs £25. It is only valid for three months. Send it, together with copies of the pages of your passports containing your details, and your original birth certificates, to the British Consulate in the Italian city where you wish to marry (see Contact details). Allow at least three months for the paperwork to be completed, as Italian bureaucracy is notoriously slow and complicated. You will be issued with a document called a *nulla osta*, which you can collect and take to the register office on your arrival in Italy.

Hotel Splendido Mare, Portofino, Italy

The Italian Embassy in London recommends that you arrange your wedding through one of their wedding specialist agencies (see Contact details) but you can do it yourself – if your have the patience and determination!

Civil weddings in Italy can only be performed in a register office. This is actually not as disappointing as it sounds, because most Italian town halls, where the register offices are located, occupy historical buildings that make an impressive setting for a wedding. Depending on the municipality the marriage is taking place in, you are required to sign a declaration of intent to marry two to five days prior to your wedding. The ceremony lasts about 30 minutes and is conducted in Italian. An interpreter will be needed throughout the ceremony. Contact the Italian Embassy (see Contact details) for information of register offices where you can book your ceremony and arrange for an interpreter.

A Roman Catholic ceremony can be performed in most cities and it will be automatically registered with the Italian authorities, and so in this instance a civil wedding is not required. However, it is purely down to the priest where you wish to marry whether he agrees to conduct the ceremony, so you'll need to make direct contact with him and find out if he needs any written details from your local parish priest in the UK. In some areas, marriages between couples of different religious denominations can be performed as long as a dispensation is obtained from your

 DREAM HOTEL
Hotel Des Bains
Lungomare Marconi 17, 30126 Venice Lido, Italy
Tel: 00 39 0415 265921
Web: www.sheraton.com

This is the ideal location from which to explore Venice, and offers a perfect retreat to escape the crowds at the end of a day's sightseeing. The charming Des Bains lies on Venice Lido and it takes just a ten-minute boat ride (which the hotel provides free of charge) across the lagoon to reach San Marco. It's a glorious place to head for in summer as there's a golden-sand beach opposite to stretch out on, or you may prefer to lie by the sparkling pool set in the pretty landscaped gardens. The rooms are large and airy, with antique pieces mixed with more modern decor. The ultimate romantic getaway, it also played a starring role in movies such as *Death in Venice* and *The English Patient*.

local parish priest. Ceremonies for other religions can also be organised, but these will not be recognised by the Italian authorities so a civil ceremony will be necessary prior to the religious ceremony. This can take place either in Italy or at home before you travel.

Weather
It can get very hot in the summer months of June to August, particularly in southern Italy and Sicily where temperatures ge well above 30°C (86°F). Further north in the mountain areas the weather is usually delightful for days on end in the summer but cool – about 4–10°C (40–50°F) – and snowy in

DREAM HOTEL
**Hotel Splendido and
Splendido Mare**
Viale Baratta 16, 16034 Portofino, Italy
Tel: 00 39 0185 267801
E-mail: reservations@splendido.net
Web: www.splendido.orient-
express.com

Set on a hillside in four acres of
romantic tropical gardens, the
Hotel Splendido overlooks the bay
of Portofino, which is just a short
stroll away. There's a poolside bar
and restaurant, the perfect place to
while away a sunny afternoon, and
the bedrooms are exquisite.
Splendido Mare is the hotel's recent
extension, which sits in the heart of
Portofino. The icing on the cake is
their private speedboat, which can
take couples out for excursions along
the coast.

the winter. Venice can be very rainy
and foggy in winter months. April
to June and early autumn are
particularly pleasant times of the
year to visit all areas of Italy.

Contact details
Italian Tourist Board
1 Princes Street, London W1R 8AY
Tel: 020 7408 1254
Fax: 020 7493 6695
E-mail: enitland@globalnet.co.uk
Websites: www.enit.it, www.piuitalia2000.it

Italian Embassy
14 Three Kings Yard, London W1Y 2EH
Tel: 020 7312 2200
Fax: 020 7312 2230
E-mail: emblondon@enbitaly.org.uk
Web: www.embitaly.org.uk

Italian wedding specialists
Weddings Made in Italy
Tel: 020 7520 0473

Italia Romantica Ltd
29 Cavendish Road, London NW6 7XR
Tel: 020 8830 2090
Web: www.italiaromantica.co.uk

Italian Connection
1st Floor Suite, 68 Gloucester Road,
London W1H 3HL
Tel: 020 7486 6890
Web: www.italian-connection.co.uk

British Consulates
Lungarno Corsini 2, 1–50123 Florence, Italy
Tel: 00 39 055 284133
Fax: 00 39 055 21912
E-mail: bcflocom@tin.it

Via San Paolo 7
1020121 Milan, Italy
Tel: 00 39 02 723001/00 39 02 723 00320
Fax: 00 39 02 8692405
Web: www.britain.it

Accademia, Dorsoduro 1051, 1–30123
Venice, Italy
Tel: 00 39 041 522 7207

DREAM HOTEL
Villa San Michele
Via Doccia 4, 50014 Fiesole, Florence,
Italy
Tel: 00 39 0555 678200
E-mail: reservations@villasanmichele.net
Web: www.lhw.com/sanmichele

The Villa occupies a former
monastery that sits on a hillside
overlooking the city of Florence – an
incredibly romantic sight, day or
night. Designed by Michelangelo,
whose artwork can still be seen there,
it is one of the best hotels in Europe
and is listed as an Italian National
Trust Monument. Most of the
beautifully furnished suites have
private terraces and some even have
private gardens, the perfect tranquil
retreat for newlyweds.

LAPLAND

What could be romantic than a wedding in the heart of the Arctic Circle in Finnish Lapland? In the winter it's a fairy-tale setting, with blankets of crisp white snow, the glowing northern lights and warm log cabins to snuggle up in. Come the summer, there are picturesque mountains to climb and valleys full of flowers to explore. Lapland really is the perfect alternative wedding destination whatever the time of year.

Travel time
Around 3 hours.

Waiting period
1 working day.

Schermachtergrond, Lapland

Documents
- Valid 10-year passports.
- Birth certificates.
- Certificates of no impediment stating your single marital status.
- Decree absolute (if divorced), marriage certificate and previous spouse's death certificate (if widowed), adoption certificate (if adopted), deed poll proof (if name changed).

Minimum age
18 years without parental consent.

Further information
All documents have to be legalised by the Legalisation Office at the Foreign and Commonwealth Office in the UK (see below for contact details). This costs around £12 per document.

Weather
Bitterly cold in the winter: temperatures are permanently below freezing, although the air is crisp and clear. There tends to be little daylight in the winter – you will feel that you are in a permanent twilight. Summer is the complete opposite, long sunny days with just a couple of hours of darkness each night.

Contact details
Finnish Tourist Board
PO Box 625, Töölönkatu 11, 00101
Helsinki, Finland
Tel: 00 11 358 941 769290
E-mail: mek@mek.fi
Web: www.finland-tourism.com

Foreign and Commonwealth Office
Old Admiralty Building, Whitehall,
London SW1A 2LG
Tel: 020 7008 1111
Web: www.fco.gov.uk

☙ DREAM HOTEL
Hotel Kakslauttanen
Fin-99830 Saariselké, Finland
Tel: 00 11 358 16 667100
Fax: 00 11 358 16 667168
E-mail: kaks-lauttanen@pp.inet.fi
Web: www.travel.fi/int/kakslauttanen

Hotel Kakslauttanen is a cosy hideaway consisting of 25 log cabins, but what's really unusual about this destination is the Igloo Village that offers the fun option of staying in a genuine snow igloo. If this takes your fancy for a first-night honeymoon location, you'll be sleeping in temperatures below zero, warm and snug in your padded sleeping bag. Alternatively, you can choose to experience the polar night sleeping under the stars in the only glass igloos in the world! There's an Ice Chapel, where you can hold your wedding ceremony, and a bar made completely of ice where you can celebrate afterwards. The hotel also offers guided Husky Safaris that include some trekking in snowshoes.

Reef Club at Westin Dragonara Resort, Malta

MALTA
Situated at the very centre of the Mediterranean, Malta is an ideal place to head if you want a wedding destination that is quiet and picturesque as well as offering sun and sand. The pretty villages, idyllic fishing harbours and beautiful temples add to its charm and it's an ideal place to honeymoon for those short of time. Malta is also an ideal two-destination wedding and honeymoon location when combined with the nearby islands of Gozo and Comino. Here you'll discover quiet coves and sandy bays with evocative names such as Paradise Bay and Golden Bay, which have long attracted couples in search of a romantic escape. Head inland and you'll discover secluded farmhouses and courtyards covered with bougainvillaea and jasmine, as well as baroque palaces and five-star hotels.

Travel time
Around 3 hours.

Waiting period
None beforehand, but you must stay for a minimum of 2 weeks.

Documents
- Valid 10-year passports.
- Birth certificates.
- Decree absolute (if divorced), marriage certificate and previous spouse's death certificate (if widowed), deed poll proof (if name changed), adoption certificate (if adopted). If divorced or widowed, an affidavit is also required, stating that you are free to marry.

DREAM HOTEL
The Westin Dragonara Resort
Dragonara Road, St Julians, Malta STJ02
Tel: 00 356 21 381 000
Web: www.starwood.com/westin

Standing on its own peninsula in St Julians, the exclusive Westin Dragonara Resort is an oasis of luxury and comfort just steps away from the shops and restaurants of downtown Malta. Every spacious guestroom boasts a spectacular view of the Mediterranean. There is an enticing array of activities, including spectacular fitness and beauty centres, water sports at two beach clubs and Malta's only casino. You can enjoy three swimming pools and learn how to scuba-dive without ever leaving the resort. To wind down from the day's adventures, sample the fusion-style cuisine at the Compass Rose restaurant or dine outdoors at The Terrace.

- Forms RZ1 and RZ2 (see below), which have to be issued within three months of the intended date to marry.
- Couples in Scotland need a certificate of no impediment.

Minimum age
18 years without parental consent. If either of you is under 18, parental consent is required in the form of a statutory declaration.

Further information
You need forms RZ1 and RZ2, which are issued by the Maltese Government and must be completed betweeen six weeks and three months before the wedding date. In Malta you will need to sign application papers and a declaration of oath in order to obtain a marriage licence from the town hall.

In Malta a civil ceremony can only take place on weekdays. The public register office in the island's capital, Valletta, is a popular location: the ceremony is conducted in English and you may include a short reading. Should you opt for a church wedding, there are around 365 to choose from, and although Malta's religion is Roman Catholic, couples from other denominations regularly hold wedding services in churches of their own religious denomination.

Weather
Hot in summer, with temperatures averaging 26°C (80°F) July to September. Much cooler – 13°C (54°F) – in winter. The best months to marry are February to June, which is after the rainy season but before temperatures soar.

Contact details
Malta Tourism Authority
Unit C, Parkhouse, 14 Northfields, London SW18 1DD
Tel: 020 8877 6990
E-mail: office.uk@visitmalta.com
Web: www.visitmalta.com

For details on civil ceremonies
Marriage Register Office
197 Merchants Street, Valletta, Malta
Tel: 00 356 21 225 291

For details on church weddings
Curia Marriages Office
PO Box 29, Valletta VLT 01, Malta

SPAIN

The British have long had a love affair with Spain, and it's easy to see why, with its great climate and tradition of relaxing siestas, not to mention the jugs of sangria at sunset. Then there are all the festivals, carnivals and religious processions, which happen all year round and greatly add to your own celebrations. And while it may have a reputation as being a 24-hour party destination in the sun, away from the over-developed Mediterranean coastal resorts you can still find a land of magical white villages, ancient castles and wonderful old Moorish palaces. Much of the countryside is beautiful and untouched and the many sierras or mountain ranges provide a rugged grandeur, but there are also many vibrant cities, such as Seville, Barcelona and Madrid.

Travel time
2–2½ hours, depending on the region you visit.

Waiting period
21 days.

Documents
- Valid 10-year passports.
- Birth certificates.
- Decree absolute (if divorced), marriage certificate and previous spouse's death certificate (if widowed).

Minimum age
18 years without parental consent.

Further information
Couples need first to obtain authorisation from the Spanish civil authorities by presenting the documents listed above, plus the

 DREAM HOTEL
Hotel La Bobadilla
Finca La Bobadilla, PO Box 144, 18300 Loja, Granada, Spain
Tel: 00 34 958 321861
Fax: 00 34 958 321810
E-mail: info@la-bobadilla.com
Web: www.la-bobadilla.com

One of the most remarkable resorts in Spain, La Bobadilla is more like a Moorish village than a hotel. It lies in the heart of Andalusia, among the legendary cities of Granada, Malaga and Sevilla, in 1,000 acres of private countryside with a private Mediterranean chapel in the grounds. The spacious rooms all lead off rambling pebbled plazas that are interconnected by a labyrinth of quaint overhanging roofs, flowering courtyards, vaulted passageways and a soaring marble colonnade. There's so much to do here that you'll want to stay on and honeymoon too; hot-air ballooning over the rolling hills and unspoilt countryside, horse riding through the flower-filled valleys, canoeing on the rivers or simply strolling hand-in-hand through the orchards listening to the birdsong. A total sanctuary.

following: an application form, which has been signed by both parties and indicates their full names, occupations, addresses and citizenship including that of their parents. This form is available from the civil registry where you want to marry (see Contact details). You will also have to provide proof that both parties are free to marry – civil registries have a document for this purpose that can be signed there when presenting the rest of the documents.

Note: All of these documents must be original certificates and must bear the official seal. All your English certificates must also be translated into Spanish (enquire at the Spanish Embassy about recognised translators) and the translation must be authenticated by the Spanish Foreign Ministry.

Spanish law now recognises Roman Catholic, Protestant, Islamic and Jewish marriages as valid in Spain without the need for a second civil marriage but regulations may vary depending on the religious denomination. Religious marriages are a matter for the relevant local church authorities in the area of the forthcoming marriage and they should therefore be consulted about their requirements – it's a good idea to do this well before your intended wedding date. To be accepted as legally valid, both in Spain and in the UK, a marriage in church must be registered with the local civil authorities. It is, therefore, important

La Bobadilla, Spain

to confirm that the particular church or priest you choose is licensed to marry and to establish the arrangements for civil registration.
Note: Paperwork can be lengthy and time-consuming and ample forward planning is necessary, especially where a marriage is to be celebrated during the summer months. Churches tend to get booked up very quickly. If you want a weekend wedding, you will need to book at least one year in advance and expect to wait at least eight weeks for your application to be processed. Formalities may vary in different registries and applicants should check in every case which documents are needed. A notice of intention to marry must be displayed on a consular notice board for a clear 21 days.

Weather

Average temperatures around 27°C (81°F) June to September and 10–15°C (50–59°F) November to March but they vary enormously, from the snowy Pyrenees to the scorching south. It can get very hot along the costas in the height of summer, and can be surprisingly cold in the interior in the winter. Most pleasant months are April to June and early autumn.

Contact details

Spanish National Tourist Office
22–23 Manchester Square, London W1M 5AP
Tel: 020 7486 8077
Web: www.tourspain.co.uk

For applications for a civil marriage

Civil Registry
Calle Pradillo 66, Madrid
Tel: 00 34 397 3700

DREAM HOTEL
Alfonso XIII

San Fernando 2, 41004 Seville, Spain
Tel: 00 34 95 4917000
Web: www.starwood.com

One of Europe's most stylish hotels, the Alfonso was named after the king who commissioned it to be built in 1928. It's a visual feast of grand archways, colourful tiled walls and the interior courtyard is an oasis of calm. The hotel's tropical gardens, dotted with orange, banana and palm trees, are a delight, and a stroll through them will reveal a beautiful Japanese restaurant and also a large outdoor pool. Bedrooms are just right for a romantic first night, each individually styled. The exquisitely appointed function rooms encircling the central courtyard are ideal for a wedding reception.

Rapadalen, Sweden

SWEDEN

Sweden is a country of endless possibilities, with a wide variety of climates, activities and scenery to suit every type of couple. It's a particularly popular destination for those who love the outdoors and adventure activities, as it offers a rugged environment that includes white-water rapids and mountains to explore. With over 12,000 miles of coastline with splendid beaches and great diving opportunities, and forests that cover 70 per cent of the country, there's no danger that you won't be able to find a picturesque spot for your wedding or honeymoon.

Travel time
Around 2 hours to Stockholm.

Waiting period
None specified.

Documents
- Valid 10-year passports.
- Birth certificates.
- Decree absolute (if divorced), marriage certificate and previous spouse's death certificate (if widowed).
- Certificate of no impediment.

Minimum age
18 years without parental consent.

Further information
The certificate of no impediment can be obtained from your local registrar in the UK. Copies of all documents should be sent to the local registration bureau in the district in which you wish to marry – contact the Swedish Embassy (see Contact details) for details of all local registrars. They will do the preparatory work and arrange for the

marriage licence to be ready upon your arrival in Sweden – providing you have all original documents with you. Both civil and religious ceremonies are possible in Sweden.

Weather
Can be bitterly cold in winter, with temperatures well below freezing. Summer months are pleasant with temperatures rising to 25°C (76°).

Contact details
Swedish Travel and Tourism Council
Sweden House, 5 Upper Montagu Street, London W1H 2AG
Tel: 0800 3080 3080 (Freephone)
E-mail: info@swetourism.org.uk
Web: www.visit-sweden.com

Embassy of Sweden
11 Montagu Place, London W1H 2AL
Tel: 020 7917 6400
E-mail:
ambassaden.london@foreign.ministry.se
Web: www.swedish-embassy.org

 DREAM HOTEL
Ice Hotel
AB Marknadsvagen 63, S–981 91 Jukkasjarvi, Sweden
Tel: 00 46 980 66800
E-mail: info@icehotel.com
Web: www.icehotel.com

At the Ice Hotel you get the opportunity to marry in a church made entirely of ice! And if that's not enough to make you want to don your snowshoes, after the ceremony you can have a drink in the Absolute Ice Bar, made – you've guessed it – entirely from ice. At night, couples get to snuggle up in reindeer skins on beds of ice. This has to be one of the most exciting destinations to marry in Europe.

SWITZERLAND
Switzerland makes a special wedding destination whatever time of year you decide to marry. In the winter months a blanket of snow covers the Alps and the lakes freeze over, while in the summer the mountain passes fill with flowers and the unspoilt countryside bursts into life. And of course, we shouldn't forget the cosmopolitan cities like Geneva, which are filled with great architecture, fabulous hotels and renowned restaurants.

Travel time
Around 1 hour 45 minutes.

Waiting period
None specified.

Documents
- Valid 10-year passports.
- Birth certificates.
- A statutory declaration and a promise of marriage form, obtainable from the Swiss Embassy (see Contact details),

---

 DREAM HOTEL
Hotel des Bergues
33 Quai des Bergues, CH 1201 Geneva, Switzerland
Tel: 00 41 22 908 7000
E-mail: info@hoteldesbergues.com
Web: www.hoteldesbergues.com

This location is as romantic as you could wish for. The hotel overlooks the waters of Lake Geneva and the picturesque Old Town, with breathtaking views of the Alps in the distance. It's extremely elegant, with plush bedrooms, superbly renovated suites and excellent restaurants. In the winter you can go skiing, in the summer take a boat out on the lake.

DREAM HOTEL
Hotel Eden Roc

Via Albarelle, CH 6612 Ascona,
Switzerland
Tel: 00 41 91 785 7143
E-mail: info@edenroc.ch
Web: www.edenroc.ch

This is an incredibly chic little
hotel on the shores of Lake
Maggiore in Ascona. Its pristine
white exterior, dazzling turquoise
swimming pool, views of the
mountains and lakes and private
beach and harbour are all very
glamorous. The bedrooms are also
very stylish, with idyllic views of the
lake, and newlyweds will enjoy the
extras, such as massages and
whirlpools, to really relax after the
big day.

must be completed and presented
to the Swiss Embassy in London
a minimum of four months
before the intended date of
marriage.
- Decree absolute (if divorced),
  death certificate of previous
  spouse (if widowed).

Note: A woman cannot remarry for
300 days after the dissolution of her
previous marriage unless she has
meanwhile given birth to a child.

Minimum age
18 years without parental consent. If
either of you is under 18, you need
proof of parental consent in the
form of a sworn affidavit.

Further information
The Swiss only recognise civil
marriages in a register office.
However, it is possible to have a
church blessing afterwards.

Before a marriage ceremony can
be performed in Switzerland the
promise of marriage must be
published at the civil registrar's
office where you plan to marry. The
promise of marriage must be made
personally on a special form
(available from the Swiss Embassy
in London) by the couple before a
registrar in Switzerland or a notary
or a solicitor in the UK. If the
promise of marriage and the
statutory declaration are made in
the UK, the notary or solicitor's
signature must be legalised by the
Foreign and Commonwealth Office
in London (see below for contact
details).

Weather
Spring is wet and cool, and April is
well known for rapidly changing
weather conditions. July to
September tend to be warm and dry,
autumn dry but cool and in winter
temperatures drop below zero. In
the Alps, there is a lot of snow in the
winter, but it can be very hot in
summer.

Contact details
Switzerland Tourism
Swiss Centre, 10 Wardour Street, London
W1D 6QF
Tel: 020 7851 1700
Web: www.switzerlandtourism.com

Embassy of Switzerland
16–18 Montagu Place, London W1H 2BQ
Tel: 020 7616 6000
E-mail: swissembassy@lon.rep.admin.ch

Chapter 4

Africa

If you're looking for that extra element of adventure, then Africa offers a wealth of possibilities. In the north, just four hours from London, Morocco has an aura of romance and mystery about it that is perfect for couples looking for something exotic. If you head further afield, you'll be spoilt for choice: a safari makes an exhilarating and unforgettable experience – who could resist exchanging vows in the glorious bush at sundown, followed by a romantic night in a luxury lodge? Or, if you want sun and sand, you can try the fabulous white-sand beaches of Kenya. Finally, South Africa has it all: first-class beaches, hotels and restaurants, breathtaking scenery in the Blue Mountains and spectacular game in the Kruger National Park. And to round off your trip, you could toast your new marriage in the beautiful wine region.

HEALTH TIPS

- There are no compulsory inoculations for Africa, but it is recommended that you are protected against hepatitis A and typhoid. In addition, you may be advised to have injections for tetanus, diphtheria, polio, hepatitis B, yellow fever, rabies and meningitis.

- Malaria is a serious problem in some lowland areas, including the Kruger National Park

Opposite: Khwai River Lodge, Botswana

BOTSWANA

Botswana's game parks and natural wonders are one of Africa's best-kept secrets, and they are incredibly romantic places to hold a wedding. Nearly 20 per cent of the country's land surface, including the remote Chobe National Park and Moremi Game Reserve, is protected as national reserves which provide magnificent settings for viewing game. Here you'll get the chance to watch large groups of elephants, prides of lion – 25-strong or more – and herds of thousands of buffalo. There's also the Okavango Delta, the world's largest inland delta, which covers an area the size of Switzerland and creates a vast oasis of flora and fauna in the most peaceful surroundings. Botswana is a true wilderness, lying under bright blue flawless skies.

Travel time

Just under 13 hours – 10 hours 45 minutes to Johannesburg, then a 2-hour connecting flight to Maun.

Waiting period

None specified.

Documents

- Valid 10-year passports.
- Birth certificates.
- Decree absolute, if divorced.

Minimum age

21 years without parental consent.

Further information

You can't apply for a marriage licence in advance, it must be purchased once you arrive in Botswana. Contact the High Commission in London for details (see Contact details). You can have either a civil or a religious ceremony in Botswana. Some of the most popular locations include Maun, Kasane, Francistown and Gaberone. More unusual destinations are the Okavango Delta or the Central Kalahar Desert.

Note: Tetanus, typhoid, paratyphoid and hepatitis are recommended inoculations for Botswana. Malaria is prevalent in northern Botswana, but cases also occur in the Kalahari area. Take a course of anti-malaria tablets as a precaution.

Weather

The best time to visit is from May through to September, when it's dry and warm without being unbearably hot.

Contact details

Botswana Department of Tourism
Petersburger Strasse 94, 10247 Berlin
Tel: 00 49 304 225 6027
E-mail: kzwiersinterface@t-online.de
Web: www.botswanatourism.org

Botswana Tourism UK
Index House, St George's Street, Ascot
SL5 7EU
Tel: 01344 636430
E-mail: botswanatourism@southern-skies.co.uk
Web: www.southern-skies.co.uk/botswana.htm

Botswana High Commission
6 Stratford Place, London W1C 1AY
Tel: 020 7499 0031

DREAM HOTEL
Sandibe Safari Lodge
Okavango Delta, Botswana
Tel: 00 267 11 809 4300
E-mail: webenquiries@ccafrica.com
Web: www.sandibe.com

Set in the heart of the sprawling Okavango Delta, a veritable Garden of Eden surrounded by the enormous Kalahari Desert, Sandibe Safari Lodge gives access to approximately 270 square kilometres of wilderness with ample opportunities for viewing big game and a wide variety of bird life. You can enjoy this first-hand by taking a guided trip in a *mokoro* (dug-out canoe) or one of the walking excursions across the delta's wonderland of waterways, floodplains, islands and forests, as well as the usual game drives. The lodge itself comprises thatched rooms with en suite dressing rooms and open-air showers, which have been sensitively designed to fit in with the landscape. Walls are airy screens, allowing the gentle Okavango breezes to cool the rooms. There are private verandas and decks, which are idyllic spots where you can lie out and view the natural wonders. At the heart of the camp, a soaring canopy of trees forms the central lounge and dining area where a fire is lit at night for the guests to gather round and discuss the day's adventures.

KENYA
If you're looking for a wedding destination with spectacular wildlife, stunning scenery and a sense of adventure, then Kenya is for you. Not only does it boast some of the best safari parks in Africa, its eastern coast is lapped by the warm Indian Ocean and has miles of white-sand beaches, making it an ideal relaxing honeymoon destination too.

Travel time
10 hours to Nairobi.

Waiting period
Under normal circumstances, residency in Kenya is 21 days. If this is not possible, a special marriage licence can be obtained beforehand by contacting the Registrar's Office in Kenya (see Contact details), in which case there is no period of residency necessary.

DREAM HOTEL
Whitesands
PO Box 90173, Mombasa, Kenya
Tel: 00 254 041 548 5926
E-mail:
reservations@whitesands.sarova.co.ke
Web: www.sarovahotels.com

As its name suggests, this lovely hotel overlooks the white-sand beach of Bamburi, just eight miles north of Mombasa, and is an ideal place to relax and get married before going on safari. There are 340 rooms, including two huge presidential suites, and lots of water sports to enjoy – jet skiing, windsurfing, pedalos, kayaking, catamarans and banana boat rides. It also has leisure cruises in glass-bottomed boats to a nearby reef where you can view the colourful coral and tropical marine life.

Documents

- Valid 10-year passports.
- Birth certificates.
- Decree absolute (if divorced), previous spouse's death certificate (if widowed), deed poll proof (if name changed).
- A statutory declaration must be obtained stating that you are both single and free to marry. This must be stamped and sealed and state the words 'solicitor', 'notary' or 'commissioner of oaths'. Hand-written documents are not accepted.

Minimum age

21 years without parental consent. If either of you is under 21 years, you must show parental consent in the form of statutory declaration stamped and signed by a solicitor.

Further information

To obtain a special marriage licence, contact the Registrar General in Nairobi (see Contact details) with copies of the necessary documentation.

You can choose from a religious ceremony in a church, a civil ceremony in a register office or – much more exciting – in a safari park. Contact the registrar General for a special licence specifying your desired place. If you want a religious ceremony, contact your chosen church for information regarding the arrangements and requirements. **Note:** No weddings are possible in Kenya from December 22 to January 5.

Weather

Kenya is very hot with temperatures averaging 29°C (85°F) May to

Mara Safari Club, Kenya

Olive stall at the soukh, Morocco

September and 32°C (90°F)
December to April, and because of
the altitude there is an increased risk
of sunburn even on cloudy days.
The rainy season runs from April
to May.

Contact details

Kenya National Tourist Office
25 Brook Mews, off Davies Street, London
W1Y 1LG
Tel: 020 7355 3144

Kenya High Commission
45 Portland Place, London, W1N 4AB
Tel: 020 7636 2371

Registrar of Marriages
Department of the Registrar General,
PO Box 30031, Nairobi, Kenya
Tel: 00 254 2 22 74 61
Fax: 00 254 2 21 56 51

Senior Assistant Registrar General
PO Box 80366, Mombasa, Kenya
Tel: 00 254 11 60 61/2

For general information

www.magicalkenya.com

DREAM HOTEL
Voi Wildlife Lodge
PO Box 30471, Tsavo National Parks,
Kenya
Tel: 00 254 336 858

Voi Wildlife Lodge lies in the
heart of the Tsavo National
Parks, which offers the chance of
seeing the Big Five – that's lion,
cheetah, leopard, buffalo and rhino
– on your honeymoon. The lodge
has only 20 rooms, which are all
large and beautifully decorated, so
it's very private, and there is a pool
and jacuzzi to relax in when you're
not out viewing game. The main
building is well appointed, with
panoramic views of the parks and
two nearby watering holes that
attract animals, particularly at
sunset, which is also the best time to
sit at Voi's open-air restaurant and
enjoy a sundowner! It's only two
hours away from the beaches of
Mombasa, so makes an ideal
addition to a sun-and-sand wedding
and honeymoon.

MOROCCO

Morocco offers something really different for British couples. So near Europe in travel time and yet so far removed culturally, its deeply rooted beliefs and traditions can still be seen and heard above the clamour of modern life. There is so much to see, including Roman ruins, ancient cities, the kasbahs and wonderfully elegant Islamic monuments. But it is perhaps the everyday way of life that makes this place so fascinating for visitors – bargaining for souvenirs in the soukhs, riding in the donkey taxis, tasting mint tea and trying out the *hammans* (steam baths). Cities like Marrakech and Fez have to be amongst the most exotic destinations you could wish for, with their date palms, pink ochre buildings and amalgam of Berber, Arab and French cultures. If you want to venture further, you can explore the snowy Atlas Mountains or even go down into southern Morocco to the edge of the Sahara Desert.

Travel time
Around 3 hours to Casablanca or Marrakech.

Waiting period
3–4 days.

Documents
- Valid 10-year passports.
- Birth certificates.
- A signed affidavit of eligibility.
- Decree absolute (if divorced), former spouse's death certificate (if widowed).

Minimum age
16 years without parental consent.

Further information

You need to have your affidavit translated into Arabic. This can be arranged through the Moroccan Embassy in the UK.

When you arrive in Morocco, take the affidavit and its translation to a government office in the area you wish to marry in to be certified. After obtaining the stamps, you should contact the local *adoul*, or priest, and provide him with all the required documents. The *adoul* will inform you of the next steps to obtain your Moroccan marriage certificate.

All types of ceremony are available and permitted. It is advisable to arrange a ceremony through your hotel.

Weather
Typically Mediterranean in the east, but modified by the Atlantic in the west. Pleasantly warm and sunny –

 DREAM HOTEL
La Mamounia
Avenue Bab Did, 40 000 Marrakech, Morocco
Tel: 00 212 44 38 86 00
E-mail: resa@mamounia.com
Web: www.mamounia.com

One of the most beautiful hotels in the world, La Mamounia is a Moroccan palace decorated in stunning Moorish and Art Deco styles that are simply breathtaking. It's set amid idyllic gardens that are almost 300 years old and surrounded by the city's twelfth-century ochre-coloured ramparts. There are lots of modern facilities to enjoy too, such as the heated swimming pool and even a casino. Weddings can be arranged on an individual basis.

DREAM HOTEL
Amanjena
Route De Ouarzazate, Km 12,
Marrakech, Morocco
Tel: 00 212 44 40 33 53
E-mail: amanjena@amanresorts.com
Web: www.amanjena.com

Amanjena is the first Amanresort on the African continent. The resort's 34 air-conditioned pavilions and six two-storey maisons are set within an oasis of palms and mature olive trees. Amanjena's rose-blush walls mirror Marrakech, whose Arabic name is *Al Medina al-Hamra* (the Red City). The resort's design emulates the old Moorish *pis* (packed earth) buildings, as well as the Berber villages that cling to the High Atlas Mountains. Each pavilion comprises a bedroom, bathroom and dressing area. The bedrooms have a high, domed ceiling, a king-size platform bed and an open fireplace. Brass lanterns and Berber carpets give a Moroccan feel, while a day bed is perfect for whiling away the hottest hours. All the suites have a mini-bar, a CD player and a TV/DVD, with a marble soaking tub in a garden setting. Each pavilion has its own private courtyard with a *minzah* (gazebo) and a fountain.

over 21°C (70°F) – for much of the year, especially along the coasts. The rainy season runs from November to April, with snow in the mountains. Inland it can be extreme, very hot in summer and very cold in winter.

Contact details
Moroccan National Tourist Office
205 Regent Street, London W1B 4HB
Tel: 020 7437 0073
E-mail: info@morocco-tourism.org.uk

SOUTH AFRICA
Many a seasoned world traveller will tell you that South Africa is the most beautiful land on the planet, with Cape Town as the shining jewel in its crown. Certainly you'd be hard pressed to find anywhere with more to offer than South Africa. It is blessed with a great year-round climate, hundreds of miles of unspoilt coastline and dramatic mountain scenery, not to mention the national parks, including the Kruger with its abundance of seriously big game, and the picturesque wine region. Your real problem will be deciding which part of this fantastic country you most want to visit, so the best plan is to

DREAM HOTEL
Roggeland Country House
Roggeland Road, Dal Josaphat Valley,
Northern Paarl, South Africa
Tel: 00 27 21 868 2501
Web: www.exploreafrica.com/roggeland

One of the most romantic hideaways in South Africa, this hotel with magnificent views sits in the picturesque wine region of the blue-purple Drakensberg Mountains. It's one of the oldest farms in the country, an eighteenth-century Cape Dutch classic with thatched roof, wood-panelled walls, wide-plank floors and a noteworthy kitchen. Dinner is a gastronomic experience, with four courses accompanied by fine wines from the area. There are 15 individual bedrooms and beautiful manicured lawns ideal for a summer wedding. While you're there, you can also try wine-tasting from the nearby vineyards or relax by the swimming pool.

marry and honeymoon there and tour around!

Travel time

Around 11 hours 30 minutes to Cape Town; around 11 hours to Johannesburg.

Waiting period

3 working days.

Documents

- Valid 10-year passports.
- Birth certificates.
- Decree absolute (if divorced), marriage certificate and previous spouse's death certificate (if widowed), adoption certificate (if adopted), deed poll proof (if name changed).

Minimum age

21 years without parental consent. If either of you is under 21, written proof of parental consent is needed.

Further information

On arrival you will need to visit the nearest Home Affairs Office to obtain a licence. These are located in all South Africa's major cities (see Contact details).

South Africa is similar to the UK in that couples are able to have a religious ceremony, including weddings in Christian churches. There is also the option of a town hall ceremony, or a ceremony at a more unusual location, such as on safari.

Weather

The best time to visit is during the spring and summer months, which run from November to April, when it's hot and dry, with an average temperature of 25°C (76°F). June, July and August tend to be colder – 16–20°C (60–68°F) – with strong winds particularly in Cape Town.

Camp's Bay, South Africa

Vineyard Hotel, South Africa

Contact details

South African Tourism Board
5–6 Alt Grove, London SW19 4DZ
Tel: 0870 155 0044
E-mail: info@southafrica.net
Web: www.southafrica.net

Regional Office of Home Affairs
Private Bag X9031, 8000 Faircape Building,
56 Barrack Street, Cape Town, 8001
South Africa
Tel: 00 27 21 462 4970
Web: www.gov.za

DREAM HOTEL
Blue Mountain Lodge
Kiepersol, Mpumalanga, South Africa
Tel: 00 27 13 737 8446
Web: www.bluemountainlodge.co.za

Set in 200 hectares of indigenous bush, forest and farmland, this pretty, ochre-washed lodge is a true 'Out of Africa' experience. Famous people who have hidden away in the landscaped gardens or sat by the pool include Nelson Mandela. You won't be able to resist the ivy-clad wedding chapel in the grounds, which you can reach along a shaded pathway lined with plumbago and sweet-smelling lavender. You can have a candlelit ceremony at dusk, and afterwards a fabulous reception on the manicured lawns. The accommodation is exceptional, whether you have a room overlooking the cobbled courtyard or one of the villas with private pool and panoramic views of the mountains.

Serengeti National Park, Tanzania

TANZANIA AND ZANZIBAR

Tanzania is home to some of Africa's most magnificent game reserves, in particular the endless plains of the Serengeti National Park, which holds some of the largest concentrations of lion, cheetah and leopard in the whole continent. The exotic island of Zanzibar, just off Tanzania's eastern coast, is a destination as exciting as it is romantic. Visitors can explore the heritage and history of the famous Stone Town, laze on the unspoilt beaches and even swim with dolphins in the seas off the south of the island. For couples looking for both adventure and time to relax in the sun, Tanzania and Zanzibar make the perfect wedding and honeymoon twin destinations.

The most romantic option is a marriage in exotic Zanzibar followed by a honeymoon in Tanzania.

Travel time

Around 10 hours to Dar Es Salaam, then a 15-minute connecting flight to Zanzibar. Alternatively, you can take the ferry, which takes 1 hour 30 minutes.

Waiting period

3 working days.

Documents

- Valid 10-year passports.
- Birth certificates.
- Decree absolute issued at least 6 months previously (if divorced), marriage certificate and previous spouse's death certificate (if widowed).

Minimum age

18 years without parental consent. If the bride is under 18, written proof of the consent of her father is needed.

Further information

If you want a religious ceremony you will require a letter from the minister of your church in the UK to say that you are single, free to marry, of good standing and have not been married before. Couples will need a confirmed place of residence (your hotel address will do) and all enquiries or application on marriage in Zanzibar must be addressed to the regional commissioner (see Contact details). You can have a civil ceremony on the beach or in hotel grounds.

Weather

It's hot all the year round with an average temperature of 27°C (81°F), but best between May and March. April and May are wetter months.

DREAM HOTEL
Breezes Beach Club
PO Box 1361, Zanzibar
Tel: 00 255 741 326595
E-mail: breezes@africaonline.co.tz
Web: www.breezes-zanzibar.com

Breezes is a beautiful 70-room resort situated on the south-east coast of Zanzibar. The hotel has a unique charm and has become renowned as a place where you can truly get away from it all. Weddings are very special, particularly the beach ceremonies at sunset, followed by a candlelit meal for two on the shore. The bedrooms are a honeymooner's dream – polished wood floors, white mosquito nets and a wonderful mix of hand-carved furniture and unique Zanzibar antiques.

Contact details

Regional Commissioner
Urban West Region, PO Box 265, Tanzania
Tel: 00 255 242 232727

Commission for Tourism
PO Box 1410, Zanzibar
Tel: 00 255 242 33485/6
E-mail:
zanzibartourism@zanzibartourism.net
Web site: www.zanzibartourism.net

Tanzania Tourist Board
PO Box 2485, Dar es Salaam
Tel: 00 255 222 111244/5
E-mail: safari@ud.co.tz or md@ttb.ud.or.tz

Tanzania High Commission
80 Borough High Street, London SE1 1LL
Tel: 020 7407 0566
Web: www.tanzania-online.gov.uk

⭑♡⭑ **Star choice**
*Pop star Sharon Corr and her husband
Gavin Bonnar chose to travel to
Tanzania's Serengati and Zanzibar as
part of their five-week honeymoon!*

 DREAM HOTEL
Kirawira Camp
Serena Central Reservation, PO Box
2551, Arusha, Tanzania
Tel: 00 255 272 508175 or 504153
E-mail: kirawira@slh.com
Web: www.slh.com/kirawira

This luxury tented camp is a
member of the Small Luxury
Hotels of the World group and is
one of the best camps in Tanzania.
Located on the Kirawira range of
hills in the western corridor of the
Serengeti, it overlooks the famous
Grumeti River, with its giant
crocodiles, and, further in the
distance, Speke's Bay, a part of Lake
Victoria. The camp, which is all
under canvas and designed to
harmonise with the natural
surroundings, consists of 25 double
tents on platforms. The beds, either
twin or king-sized, are mosquito
netted and covered in bright
patchwork covers. Each en-suite
bathroom contains a generous
selection of Floris goodies including
blissful aromatherapy oils, a robe
and big, soft, white towels. A large
tented veranda allows you to sit
outside and gaze at the lovely views,
and a covered terrace flanking the
main lounge frames vistas across the
plains to the misty-blue Bunda Hills
rising in the distance. A thoughtfully
placed telescope allows you to pick
out game and it's the ideal spot to
enjoy afternoon tea or a
pre-dinner drink.

CHAPTER 5

THE INDIAN OCEAN

If you hanker after nothing more than blue skies, warm seas and white sandy beaches, then you definitely need to pay a visit to the islands of the Indian Ocean. Rich in culture, incredibly lush and very friendly, they make a perfect long-haul wedding destination. The 115 islands of the Seychelles have long been regarded as one of the earth's most desirable retreats, not least because of their tropical vegetation and wonderful variety of bird and animal life. But if you're after a little more glamour and sophistication, then try the island of Mauritius. Its shores are lined with five-star hotels, yachts and pristine beaches, while inland you'll marvel at the mountains and waterfalls. Sri Lanka is a popular wedding destination for Brits as the ceremony is quick and easy to arrange and there are lots of fun options – you can even arrive at the ceremony on the back of an elephant. It also makes a perfect honeymoon spot, as there are lots of hotels, restaurants and bars to enjoy as well as the beautiful scenery. Be warned, however, this tropical paradise is hot and humid, with a monsoon season. If you decide to save money and arrive out of season, you are likely to experience some exceptionally heavy downpours.

HEALTH TIPS

- There are no compulsory vaccination requirements for countries in the Indian Ocean. However, you should be protected against hepatitis A and typhoid and it may also be advisable to have inoculations against polio, hepatitis B, tuberculosis, diphtheria and rabies.
- Malaria is a problem in low-lying rural areas.

MAURITIUS

This island in the Indian Ocean is a hugely popular wedding and honeymoon destination for British couples, thanks to its pristine white-sand beaches, friendly people and fine hotels. It is blessed with a lush landscape inland, including soaring mountains, deep, still lakes and swaying sugar cane plantations. On the coast, the waters are incredibly clear and warm and the beaches are truly exceptional. Not that it's simply a desert island paradise: Mauritius has a thriving capital, Port Louis, where there are great shops, bars and restaurants to enjoy.

Travel time

12 hours to Plaisance airport.

Waiting period

24 hours.

Documents

- Valid 10-year passports.
- Birth certificates.
- Decree absolute (if divorced). If you are getting married within 10 months of the divorce pronouncement you will need your local doctor's certificate of non-pregnancy.
- Marriage certificate and previous spouse's death certificate (if widowed).

Minimum age

18 years without parental consent. If either of you is under 18, proof of parental consent in the form of an affidavit, stamped by a notary, must be produced.

Further information

The Civil Status Act states that marriage of non-residents can take

DREAM HOTEL
Le Saint Géran Hotel, Spa and Golf Club
Belle Mare, Mauritius, Indian Ocean
Tel: 00 230 401 1688
E-mail: infostg@sunresort.com

A dazzling retreat set in 60 acres of tropical gardens, one side facing the warm Indian Ocean and the other a sheltered lagoon, all surrounded by a soft, white-sand beach. It's an exclusive place to get married, so you definitely won't find more than one ceremony a day here, and they are arranged on an individual basis. There are 148 suites and 14 ocean suites so this is a sizeable resort, but the layout ensures it's incredibly private. Famous faces seen at the Saint Géran Hotel have included Prince William, Geri Halliwell and Pierce Brosnan.

place the day following the publication of marriage banns. However, the couple must obtain a certificate issued by the Prime Minister's office and given to the Registrar of Civil Status officer

Sun, sea and palms in Mauritius

DREAM HOTEL
Royal Palm Hotel

Grand Baie, Mauritius, Indian Ocean
Tel: 00 230 209 8300
E-mail: royalpalm@bchot.com
Web: www.lhw.com/royalpalm

Overlooking the glorious Grand Sable Beach in the north-west of the island, this oasis of luxury provides a tranquil setting for couples who want to be pampered – staff outnumber guests by three to one! Weddings here are very intimate and low key; you can't have a party bigger than six. Only 30 metres from the beach and facing the lagoon, the 84 suites and rooms are very private, spacious and elegantly decorated, which is why they attract royalty and celebrities looking to escape the crowds.

stating that you are neither a citizen nor a resident of Mauritius. This can be obtained beforehand by sending a request to the Registrar of Civil Status (see Contact details). The document must be accompanied by copies of both your birth certificates as well as photocopies of the pages containing your personal details pages in your passports.

If you want a religious ceremony, in addition to the documents listed above, you will also need your christening certificates and a 'certificate of good morality' from your respective parish priests, specifying that you are both free to marry and not divorced. Roman Catholics wishing to get married in Mauritius are requested to contact the Port Louis diocese to obtain the necessary information (telephone 00 230 208 3068).

If you decide not to marry in one of Mauritius's lovely churches, you can choose where your ceremony takes place from a number of beautiful settings, from under a palm tree in the garden of your hotel to on a jetty in the sea or even on a boat. If you are having a civil ceremony you must send copies of your documents in advance to The Registry, Civil Status Division (see Contact details), and you must take the originals with you for submission on your wedding day.

Weather

Even the supposedly cooler season, which runs from April to November, is pleasantly warm with temperatures only dropping to about 24°C (75°F). The summer months of November to April can get very hot, and there is some risk of cyclones in January and February. There is a high level of rainfall inland.

Contact details

Mauritius Tourism Promotion Authority
32–33 Elvaston Place, London SW7 5NW
Tel: 020 7584 3666
Fax: 020 7225 1135
E-mail: mtpa@btinternet.com
Web: www.mauritius.net

The Registry, Civil Status Division
E Anquetil Building, Sir S Ramgoolam Street, Port Louis, Mauritius, Indian Ocean
Tel: 00 230 201 1727

Registrar of Civil Status
7th Floor, Emmanuel Anquetil Building, Port Louis, Mauritius, Indian Ocean
Tel: 00 230 201 1727
Fax: 00 230 211 2420

SEYCHELLES

The islands of the Seychelles are jaw-droppingly gorgeous; lush forests, exotic wildlife, flaming sunsets and great beaches are all part of this territory. If you're looking for lots of amenities to go with this tropical Utopia, then head for Mahé, the largest and most popular of the 115 islands that make up the archipelagos. Here you'll discover lots of smart hotels as well as breathtaking scenery; soaring mountains carpeted with ancient forests and dazzling white powder-sand beaches are plentiful. If you want somewhere even more laid back, try Mahe's tiny neighbours such as Praslin, Bird and Frégate islands.

Travel time

Around 13 hours to Mahé or Praslin.

 DREAM HOTEL
Frégate Island
Seychelles, Indian Ocean
Tel: 00 248 28 22 85
E-mail: fregate@seychelles.net
Web: www.fregate.com

Situated 35 miles east of Mahé, Frégate Island offers maximum privacy and exclusivity in every respect. This small private paradise features only 16 luxuriously appointed villas, seven dream beaches, crystal waters, and flora and fauna that boast some of the rarest species on earth. Its breathtaking natural beauty, exquisite gourmet cuisine and complete range of water sports and recreational activities make it a winner for anyone looking for the ultimate wedding and honeymoon getaway.

Waiting period

11 days. However, this can be exempted by applying for a special licence, which will be issued two days after application. Your marriage can be solemnised immediately afterwards.

Documents

- Valid 10-year passports.
- Birth certificates.
- A certified affidavit declaring that there is no lawful impediment why you cannot marry.
- Decree absolute (if divorced), marriage certificate and previous spouse's death certificate (if widowed), deed poll proof (if name changed).

Minimum age

18 years without parental consent. If the bride is under 18, she must have the written consent of her father. If her parents are not married, then the consent of the mother will be accepted.

Further information

You can make arrangements for obtaining a special marriage licence with the senior officer of the Civil Status Office (see Contact details). You must provide the date of your holiday, the name of the hotel where the ceremony is to take place and a preferred date (give alternatives). The licence costs SR100 (£10). Your hotel must also confirm that your chosen date is acceptable and advise a suitable

 Star choice
The Seychelles' off-the-beaten-track solitude attracts stars such as heart-throb Brad Pitt and his wife, actress Jennifer Aniston.

DREAM HOTEL
Banyan Tree
Mahé, Seychelles, Indian Ocean
Tel: 00 248 383500
E-mail: reservations@banyantree.com
Web: www.banyantree.com

Situated on beautiful Intendance Bay, 36 luxuriously furnished villas nestle amid exotic flora and fauna and command magnificent views of the ocean. Villas boast private swimming pools and outdoor pavilions. The two gourmet restaurants offer Thai, Asian, European and creole cuisine, while the La Varangue bar serves cocktails and snacks all day. Truly an island paradise.

time of day. Send certified copies of the above documentation, and take the originals with you when you travel. The senior officer of the Civil Status Office will confirm the date of your wedding, fee details and whether further documentation is required.

Bonnaire, Seychelles

If your ceremony is to take place at the Civil Status Office, the time and date can be booked in advance, but you must report there on arrival with your original documents. Weddings in the office are normally performed on Tuesday and Thursday mornings only, in the presence of two witnesses.

It is possible to have a ceremony performed on a beach but this is not normal procedure and would have to be arranged directly with the Civil Status Office prior to your travel date. Allow at least two months to process the documentation and make the necessary arrangements.

Most couple are married at their hotel in the gardens or on the beach although it is possible to arrange a wedding on a yacht or in other locations. Religious ceremonies can be arranged but not through the Civil Status Office. Seychelles law does not recognise religious ceremonies but couples can have a civil ceremony followed by a religious ceremony. Couples should ask their UK parish priest to make direct contact with a priest in the Seychelles. All the other formalities detailed above must be complied with. Contact the Seychelles Tourist Office for details of churches.

Weather
The islands enjoy a tropical climate all year round: as they are situated outside the cyclone belt, there are no extremes of weather. The temperature seldom drops below 25°C (78°F) or rises above 33°C (92°F). It is an ideal holiday destination at any time of year.

Contact details

Seychelles Tourist Office
36 Southwark Bridge Road, London SE1 9EU
Tel: 020 7202 6363
Web: www.seychelles.uk.com

Senior Officer of the Civil Status
Office
PO Box 430, Victoria, Mahé, Seychelles,
Indian Ocean
Tel: 00 248 224030
Fax: 00 248 225474

Elephant ride, Sri Lanka

SRI LANKA

The teardrop-shaped isle of Sri
Lanka is one of the most popular
places for Brits to marry abroad and
for good reason. It's an incredibly
beautiful island, just south of the
Indian subcontinent, with a huge
variety of things to see and do.
Sandy beaches, dense jungles, hills
to trek in and bustling coastal
villages to explore. Its heady
combination of spices, temples and
flora and fauna make for an exotic
mix. It's also just an hour's flight
from the magical Maldives, perfect
for a two-destination honeymoon!

You can decide to go for a
traditional religious Sri Lankan
ceremony with music from a
Calypso band, dancers and
drummers and leave your ceremony
on the back of an elephant or in a
bullock cart. Another alternative is
to marry at sunset on a moonlit

DREAM HOTEL
Closenberg Hotel

11 Closenberg Rd, Galle, Sri Lanka
Tel: 00 94 932 241

A real hidden treasure of a hotel
that's well off the beaten track
and ideal for couples wanting to
escape the crowds. It's an old
colonial building, originally built as
a private residence about 150 years
ago and furnished with many pieces
of original antique furniture. It's
surrounded by a tropical garden full
of beautiful flowers and is on an
elevated location on a peninsula at
the border of the city of Galle.
There's a sandy beach below, which
takes about five minutes to reach.
There are only 21 rooms, so it's
small and intimate.

beach or during the day in the garden of your hotel.

Travel time
Around 11 hours and 15 minutes.

Waiting period
4 working days.

Documents
- Valid 10-year passports.
- Birth certificates.
- An affidavit signed by a solicitor, stating that neither of you has been previously married and that there is no legal objection to the marriage.
- Decree absolute (if divorced), marriage certificate and previous spouse's death certificate (if widowed), deed poll proof (if name changed).

Minimum age
21 years without parental consent. If either of you is under 21, a statutory declaration of parental consent, plus legalisation and certification of documents, will be required.

Further information
All documents must be in English. You should take the originals of all the necessary documents to the Civil Status Officer in the area where you wish to marry (see Contact details) and must also provide your full names and addresses, those of your parents and details of your professions.

Weather
Consistently hot – 30°C (86°F) or above – all year round. Rainy months are May to June and October to November.

Contact details
Sri Lanka Tourist Board
22 Regent Street, London SW1Y 4QD
Tel: 020 7930 2627
Fax: 020 7930 9070
E-mail: srilanka@cerbernet.co.uk
Web: www.lanka.net/ctb

Sri Lanka High Commission
13 Hyde Park Gardens, London W2 2LU
Tel: 020 7262 1841
Fax: 020 7262 7970
E-mail: lancom@easynet.co.uk

 DREAM HOTEL
Blue Water
Thalpitiya, Wadduwa, Sri Lanka
Tel: 00 94 34 35067
E-mail: bluewater@sltnet.lk
Web: www.lanka.net/jetwing/bluewater/index.html

Situated in 14 acres of grounds in the coastal town of Wadduwa, this hotel is known for its great service and its special weddings. There are lots of packages and locations to choose from, and a free candlelit dinner for newlyweds. The 96 rooms and four suites are simple but luxurious and all have sea view with a private balcony or terrace. There are all the facilities that you'd expect from a top resort, including a large swimming pool, long sandy beach, gym, tennis courts and even a nightclub.

CHAPTER 6

THE CARIBBEAN

The Caribbean is all of your tropical island dreams rolled into one, so is the perfect place to travel to get married if you're after sun, sea and sand. While the 30-plus islands all have the prerequisite golden beaches fringed with coconut palms, each one is unique, so you'll need to investigate which is the perfect wedding isle for you. From larger and well-known islands such as Cuba and Jamaica, with their lush interiors and vibrant vibe, to the tiny destinations of Anguilla and Mustique, there is an island to suit every couple.

The weather is one of the great attractions of the area. Being a tropical region, the temperatures are constant and hot all the year round, so you need not take anything more than a light sweater in case it's breezy in the evening. However, be warned: one of the other characteristics of the tropics is that it can – and does – rain at any time. All that lush vegetation isn't there by chance! The showers, though usually short, can be very heavy, and it can rain for days on end, so don't assume blue skies are absolutely guaranteed. Check carefully for the wettest months on each island, and be prepared.

HEALTH TIPS

- There are no compulsory inoculations for the Caribbean, but it is recommended to have jabs for tetanus, typhoid, polio, hepatitis A and B, diphtheria and TB.
- Malaria is not a problem but mosquito repellent is a good idea.

ANGUILLA

This is the place to head if you like the idea of a beach wedding. It's a tiny, flat island just 16 miles long and three miles wide, which has some of the best stretches of shimmering white sand in the Caribbean. Marketed as 'tranquillity wrapped in blue', Anguilla is surrounded by luminous turquoise seas and is a watersports-lover's paradise. Breezy trade winds make sailing a favourite, along with canoeing, windsurfing, waterskiing and parasailing. The island is also popular for underwater sports such as snorkelling and diving as it's surrounded by pristine reefs, wrecks and beautiful marine life. Hydrophobes won't lack for something to do either: you can take out a couple of horses for a ride, hike to caves or to the lush rainforest, visit an art gallery or museum, or go birdwatching. Despite its size, the standard of hotels and restaurants is exceptionally high, and most of the larger resorts offer wedding packages.

Travel time

About 8 hours to Antigua, plus a 30-minute connecting flight to Anguilla.

Waiting period

2 days.

Documents

- Valid 10-year passports.
- Birth certificates.
- Decree absolute (if divorced), marriage certificate and previous spouse's death certificate (if widowed).

All documents must be in English.

Dancing on the beach, Anguilla

Opposite: Swimming in Aruba

DREAM HOTEL
Cap Juluca
PO Box 240, Maundays Bay, Anguilla,
Leeward Islands, British West Indies
Tel: 00 1 264 497 6666
Web: www.capjuluca.com

Situated on the south-western coast of Anguilla and overlooking the mountains of St Maarten, Cap Juluca occupies 179 acres of land and inland waters. There are lots of pretty wedding sites, including the beach and a pavilion in the landscaped gardens. While situated only 15 minutes by boat from the myriad of shops, restaurants, gambling, and international flavours of Dutch and French St Maarten, Cap Juluca remains the essence of tranquillity. There are 18 separate Moorish-style beachfront villas, and they are furnished beautifully with white walls, giant beds and bathtubs built for two! Newlyweds will appreciate the complimentary continental breakfast, served daily on your private terrace.

Minimum age
18 years without parental consent.

Further information
If you are having a religious ceremony, you'll need written permission from your local church or priest to say that you are free to marry. The marriage licence and stamp duty cost US $284 (£170), which is reduced if one partner resides on the island for a minimum of 15 days before the wedding.

Weather
The best time to visit is December to March when the temperatures are hot – average 26°C (80°F) – and

 Star choice
Friends' actress Courtney Cox and her husband actor David Arquette honeymooned in Anguilla at the luxury Cap Juluca hotel.

there is less chance of rain. The island tends to be very quiet from mid-September to the end of October, the rest of the year is more lively.

Contact details
Anguilla Tourist Board
River Communications, Unit 8a, Oakwood House, 414–422 Hackney Road, London E2 7SY
Tel: 020 7729 8003
E-mail: anguilla4info@aol.com
Web: www.anguilla-vacation.com

 DREAM HOTEL
Malliouhana Hotel
PO Box 173, Meads Bay, Anguilla,
Leeward Islands, British West Indies
Tel: 00 1 264 4976111
E-mail: malliouhana@anguillanet.com
Web: www.malliouhana.com

Malliouhana Hotel is situated on a bluff at the northern point of Meads Bay, a mile-long stretch of white sand lapped by clear blue water, which is the perfect place to exchange your wedding vows. Another popular option is a sunset ceremony at the end of a rocky promontory set out to sea. The hotel's 55 rooms and suites are all spacious and most overlook the sea. Facilities include freshwater pools, an exercise room, water sports, tennis courts, boutique, spa and a boat service. Malliouhana, which is the old name for Anguilla, also has a romantic restaurant that overlooks Meads Bay, the ideal place to celebrate your marriage.

ANTIGUA AND BARBUDA

Antigua is famous for the fact that it has 365 public beaches – one for each day of the year – a dream for couples seeking to have a beach wedding! It sits in the middle of the Leeward Islands in the Eastern Caribbean and is only about 14 miles long and 11 miles wide. Its coral reefs offer some of the best diving in the Caribbean. The southern and eastern coasts of Antigua and virtually the entire coastline of Barbuda are surrounded by shelves, providing excellent conditions for spectacular shallow diving and snorkelling. One of Antigua's best-known offshore sites, Cades Reef, is now partly contained in a designated underwater park. There is little or no current in most places, the water temperature averages about 26°C (80°F) and tropical marine plants and animals are diverse and plentiful.

If you want a two-destination wedding and honeymoon, then a trip to the fascinating little island of Barbuda, just off the coast of Antigua, is recommended. Barbuda is one of those very few islands in the Caribbean that is so undeveloped as to seem positively deserted at times – and probably will remain so for some time. With the exception of the guests of the island's small number of hotels, the main inhabitants you'll see here are birds – the island boasts the Caribbean's finest bird sanctuary. Barbuda's seemingly endless white and pink-sand beaches are left to the peaceful wanderings of those lucky enough to sojourn here. Activities

 DREAM HOTEL
Jumby Bay Resort Villas and Suites
PO Box 243, St John's, Antigua, West Indies
Tel: 00 1 268 462 6000
E-mail: jumbybay@rosewoodhotels.com
Web: www.hotelsdeluxe.com/JumbyBay

The all-inclusive Jumby Bay Resort is set on a paradise island just two miles off the coast of Antigua, which you reach by private ferry. Nearly one-third of the secluded, 300-acre island is taken up with the 50 suites and villas of the resort, so it's an ideal place for couples seeking lots of privacy. You can choose from a variety of locations for your wedding ceremony, but the most popular are barefoot beach ceremonies. It is perfect for honeymooners too, with three superb, white-sand beaches to laze on. Nearby Pasture Bay Beach is home to endangered turtle species.

are appropriately relaxed, including beachcombing (on the north-eastern Atlantic coast), fishing and hunting and, at the island's resorts, golf, tennis, snorkelling, diving, or simply soaking up the sun.

Travel time
Around 8 hours to Antigua, plus a 20-minute connecting flight to Barbuda.

Waiting period
3 days.

Documents
- Valid 10-year passports.
- Birth certificates.
- Affidavit confirming single status, which can be bought in Antigua for US $50 (£30).

Galley Bay, Antigua

- Decree absolute showing coloured stamp (if divorced), marriage certificate and previous spouse's death certificate (if widowed), deed poll proof (if name changed), adoption certificate (if adopted).

Minimum age

18 years without parental consent. If either of you is under 18, parental consent in the form of an affidavit obtained in the UK will be required.

Further information

The necessary legal documents must be presented to the Ministry of Legal Affairs in St Johns, Antigua, where you will be asked to fill out an application form and pay a fee of US $150 (£90). You then need to proceed to the High Court, located just around the corner on High Street, to meet with a marriage officer. The officer will review your application, issue a special marriage licence, which costs US $75 (£45), and agree the date, time and place for the ceremony. You must then return to the Ministry of Legal Affairs to file the application form.

After that, you are free to marry anywhere on the island.

Weather

Warm and sunny during the winter months, with occasional storms from August to October. Temperatures generally range from an average of 24°C (75°F) in the winter to about 29°C (85°F) in the

 DREAM HOTEL
Curtain Bluff
PO Box 288, Antigua, West Indies
Tel: 00 1 268 462 8400
Web: www.curtainbluff.com

Curtain Bluff sits on a private peninsula on Antigua's picturesque south coast, and is a romantic's dream. Everything here is geared towards couples in love, from the hammocks for two dotted around the grounds to the private balconies overlooking the sea, not to mention two pristine beaches. Everything about this pink and white resort is simply perfect, from the extensive wine cellar to the flower displays to the restaurant. Wedding ceremonies can take place in any part of the resort, including a gazebo in the gardens or on the beach.

DREAM HOTEL
Palmetto Beach Hotel
Barbuda Island, Antigua, West Indies
Tel: 0800 2000 3456
E-mail: info@palmettohotel.com
Web: www.palmettohotel.com

This gorgeous slice of paradise has just 21 junior suites and one-bedroom villas (ideal for honeymooners), all facing the 20 miles of beach. There aren't lots of weddings here, so you can be sure that yours will be tailor made and pretty special. All the suites have two queen-size beds, and covered verandas with chairs to relax in. The restaurant and bar are located on the poolside terrace, close to the beach and with an enchanting view of the Caribbean Sea. The Italian chef prepares excellent international cuisine and the service at this hotel is of an exceptionally high standard.

summer. These are the sunniest of the Eastern Caribbean islands, and the north-east trade winds are nearly constant, dropping only in September. Humidity is low all the year round.

Contact details

Antigua and Barbuda High Commission and Tourist Office
15 Thayer Street, London W1U 3JT
Tel: 020 7486 7073/5
Fax: 020 7486 1466
E-mail: antbar@msn.com
Web: www.interknowledge.com

Ministry of Legal Affairs
Redcliffe Street, St Johns, Antigua, West Indies
Tel: 00 1 268 462 0017

For general information

Web: www.antigua-barbuda.com/tourists

ARUBA

The island of Aruba sits just 15 miles off the north coast of Venezuela and has a fascinating mix of South American and European, Far East and Caribbean influences. It's the place to head if you're looking for a wedding destination with lots to see and do as well as fabulous beaches.

Oranjestad is the historical Dutch capital city on the southern coast where the tall multicoloured houses of Wilheminastraat combine carved wooden doors and traditional Dutch tiles with airy open galleries and sloping, Aruban-style roofs. Along the wharf, merchants come to sell fresh fish and produce right off the boats every morning. Depending on the time of year, you could also find yourself in the middle of Carnival, a summertime festival, the New Year's fireworks, or even a parade in honour of the Queen! Aruba is also well known for its glitzy and glamorous casinos, some of which stay open 24 hours, so you can get married and then head for the bright lights!

Aruba sunset

DREAM HOTEL
Wyndham Aruba Beach Resort and Casino
JE Irausquin Boulevard 77, Aruba, Dutch Caribbean
Tel: 00 297 5864 466
E-mail: info@arubawyndham.com
Web: www.arubawyndham.com

Nestled on the soft, white sands of Aruba's Palm Beach and surrounded by lush, landscaped gardens, Wyndham Aruba Beach Resort and Casino rests on the island's west coast. Here you can have your wedding ceremony and reception under one roof for the ultimate convenience. This hotel offers pretty much anything you desire for your wedding and honeymoon, from rehearsal dinners to a picturesque ceremony setting in the gardens.

Travel time
11 hours.

Waiting period
None specified.

Documents
- Valid 10-year passports.
- Apostile (a special official document stating that you are free and eligible to marry).
- Birth certificates with raised seal.
- Divorce certificate (if divorced), marriage certificate and former spouse's death certificate (if widowed).

Minimum age
18 years without parental consent.

Further information
You must submit the apostile, birth certificates and copies of your passports and your witnesses'

passports one month before the wedding to the Bureau of Vital Statistics, where a government official will prepare your paperwork. Aruba only recently started to allow British couples to marry there, so the island is still developing its wedding industry.

Note: For the marriage to be legally binding, all couples must first have a civil ceremony. You can then have a blessing (which can be just like a wedding ceremony) on a beach, boat or hotel overlooking the sea.

Weather
Aruba is outside the hurricane belt and sunny and hot all year round. There is no rainy season.

Contact details
Aruba Tourism Authority
Saltmarsh Partnership, The Copperfields, 25 Copperfield Street, London SE1 0EN
Tel: 020 7928 1600

 DREAM HOTEL
Bucuti Beach
PO Box 1299, Eagle Beach, Aruba, Dutch Caribbean
Tel: 00 297 583 1100
Web: www.bucuti.com

The Bucuti Beach is made for honeymooners and couples in love. A white, 64-room hacienda-style hotel right on one of the island's best beaches, a stretch of white palm-fringed sand so perfect you'll never want to leave – and it's also the ideal spot for a blessing. The rooms are colourful, in keeping with the tropical nature of the island, there's a gym and a freshwater pool to keep you cool and next door there's the Alhamba Casino if you fancy a flutter.

BAHAMAS

The Bahamas consists of over 700 islands of varying sizes scattered across more than 100,000 square miles of the Atlantic Ocean about 150 miles east of Florida. There's a tremendous choice of wedding destinations to choose from, although the most popular and organised destination catering for foreign ceremonies is the island of New Providence, home to the islands' capital Nassau. In times gone by, Nassau was an international playground for the rich. Today, the first city of the Bahamas attracts not only the affluent of the world but also honeymooners of every class and culture, especially from America. Visitors can explore its narrow streets and the old British forts, climb the Queen's Staircase and wander through outlying villages dating back to the days of slavery and beyond.

Paradise Island, a long, narrow barrier island connected to Nassau by a toll bridge, is a world of hotels, restaurants and exciting nightlife, but there are also unspoiled pockets where visitors can enjoy the sea and the beaches without having to travel too far from the bustling streets of the city.

Travel time
Around 9 hours to Nassau.

Waiting period
1 day.

Documents
- Valid 10-year passports.
- Birth certificates.
- Decree absolute (if divorced), marriage certificate and former spouse's death certificates (if widowed).
- If either of you has never been married before, an affidavit certifying this fact must be sworn before a notary or other person

 DREAM HOTEL
Ocean Club
PO Box N–4777, Nassau, Bahamas
Tel: 00 1 254 713 7323
Web: www.oceanclub.com

A legend in the hotel world, Ocean Club nestles on Paradise Island across the bridge from Nassau. Once a private estate, it lies between miles of pristine beach and exquisite gardens inspired by the romantic grandeur of Versailles. Fragrant blossoms of hibiscus and bougainvillaea, along with hand-laid rock ridges and stone steps, ascend the terraced garden decorated with bronze and marble statues. The 35 acres of seaside grounds centre on a two-storey colonial mansion built in the late 1930s. Today, following a $100-million restoration and expansion, the resort offers a host of amenities and facilities, including weddings in the grounds, on the beach and in the main resort.

Supermodel Cindy Crawford and her millionaire boyfriend Rande Gerber chose to marry at the Ocean Club. They took over the whole resort and invited friends and family to stay for the beach ceremony.

 Star choice
You'll be in good company on the Bahamian island of Eleuthera – famous faces who have holidayed there include Rolling Stone Keith Richards and film stars Julia Roberts, Robin Williams, Susan Sarandon and Tim Robbins.

DREAM HOTEL
Pink Sands
Harbour Island, Eleuthera, Bahamas
Tel: 00 1 242 333 2030
E-mail:
reservations@islandoutpost.com
Web: www.islandoutpost.com

Situated on Harbour Island amid 18 acres overlooking the most beautiful stretch of pink-sand beach in the world, Pink Sands has lots of colonial charm and is a popular resort for weddings and honeymoons. The famous beaches were created by thousands of years of red coral mixing with the white sand, and the result is so pretty you'll want all of your wedding photographs to be taken on the beach! Travelling around the island is easy since it is only 3½ miles long and ½ mile wide and has a resident population of just 2,000. Most visitors use bicycles or golf carts to explore.

authorised to administer in the Bahamas. The declaration must accompany the application for the marriage licence.

Sailing in the Bahamas

Minimum age

18 years without parental consent. If either of you is under 18, written proof of parental consent is required.

Further information

Both parties must be in the Bahamas at the time of the application. The parties must produce evidence of the date of their arrival in the Bahamas (i.e. an immigration card, which you receive when you enter the Bahamas). The fee for a marriage licence is US $40 (£24).

Note: Marriage licences are issued at the office of the Registrar General in Nassau (see Contact details). This office is open Monday to Friday, 9.30 am to 4.30 pm, except on Bahamian public holidays.

 DREAM HOTEL
Sandals Royal Bahamian Resort and Spa
PO Box 39, CB 13005, Cable Beach, Nassau, Bahamas
Tel: 00 1 242 327 6400
Web: www.sandals.com

Located on Nassau's renowned Cable Beach, 15 minutes from Nassau International Airport, Sandals Royal Bahamian was created especially for couples in love, honeymooners and wedding parties. It's ideal for those on a tight budget who want to experience the wonder of the Bahamas – you can have a free wedding ceremony if you spend five nights or more at the hotel as part of your honeymoon. The package will include bouquet and cake and all the basics, and is the ideal solution if you're looking for a hassle-free wedding without all the trimmings.

Weather

Regarded as one of the most delightful climates in the world. Frost is unknown, winter temperatures are warm but summer temperatures rarely go above 32°C (90°F) and there are always fresh sea breezes. There can be heavy rain showers at any time, with wet days most likely in June, September and October.

Contact details

Registrar General of the Bahamas
PO Box N–532, Nassau, Bahamas

Bahamas Tourist Office
3 The Billings, Walnut Tree Close,
Guildford, Surrey GU1 4UL
Tel: 01483 448900
Web: www.bahamas.com

BARBADOS

One of the most popular Caribbean islands, Barbados is a glorious fusion of West Indian and English cultures, which makes it a charming wedding destination. Its combination of sophisticated resorts, great beaches and consistent good weather – there hasn't been a hurricane there for years – have helped to make it a thriving destination. It's also a favourite playground of the jet set, where you're quite likely to end up lying on a sunlounger next to Naomi Campbell. There's a glitzier, more cosmopolitan feel to Barbados than some of the smaller islands, and it boasts some of the best restaurants in the Caribbean, such as celebrity favourite The Cliff, and also has a good nightlife scene. It's the ideal

Coral Reef Club, St James, Barbados

place for couples looking for a little bit of glamour on their wedding and honeymoon.

Travel time
Just under 9 hours.

Waiting period
1 day.

Documents
- Valid 10-year passports.
- Birth certificates.
- Decree absolute (if divorced), marriage certificate and previous spouse's death certificate (if widowed), adoption certificate

 DREAM HOTEL
Coral Reef Club
St James, Barbados
Tel: 00 1 246 422 2372
E-mail: coral@caribsurf.com
Web: www.coralreefbarbados.com

Set amidst 12 acres of beautifully landscaped gardens on the calm west coast of Barbados, the family-owned Coral Reef Club is one of the finest places to tie the knot in the Caribbean. A sweeping driveway leads you up to the splendid colonial-style main house, from where you can catch a glimpse of the pretty gardens and picturesque, secluded bay. The bedrooms are bright and airy, and there are two swimming pools offering an oasis from the day's heat as do the soaring trees fringing the white sandy beach where a wide range of complimentary water sports is available.

(if adopted), deed poll proof (if name changed).

Minimum age
18 years without parental consent.

Further information
It is very easy to get married in Barbados. An application for a marriage licence must be made by both parties in person at the office of the Ministry of Home Affairs. You must take all the documents listed above with you. You then

 DREAM HOTEL
Cobblers Cove
Speightstown, St Peter, Barbados
Tel: 00 1 246 422 2291
E-mail: reservations@cobblerscove.com
Web: www.cobblerscove.com

Cobblers Cove is located on the north-west coast of Barbados and overlooks a white-sand beach and calm, clear blue waters. It's all very romantic, with gardens full of hibiscus and bougainvillaea and an exceptional honeymoon suite with a plunge pool and panoramic views of the ocean. The other 40 spacious suites are also impressive, and boast their own living areas, with balcony or patio, giant beds and bathrooms with lots of extras such as fluffy towelling robes and luxury toiletries. If you can drag yourself away from the beach, there are lots of water sports to indulge in, including waterskiing, windsurfing and snorkelling. The hotel is within easy walking distance of Speightstown, which has recently been revived and is now the home of a brand-new luxury marina. There are also some excellent restaurants in the area and some fine examples of Barbadian architecture.

have to take all your documents to the Ministry of Justice and Public Safety (see Contact details) where you'll obtain your licence, which costs US $75.76 (£45) and stamp duty of US $12.62 (£8). There are lots of places to tie the knot in Barbados, including restaurants, such as The Tides with its fabulous oceanfront location.

Weather
Average year-round temperature 31°C (88°F). The driest time is the winter, i.e. December to March.

Contact details
Barbados Tourism Authority
263 Tottenham Court Road, London
W1T 7LA
Tel: 020 7636 9448
E-mail: btauk@barbados.org
Web: www.barbados.org

Ministry of Justice and Public Safety
5th Floor, General Post Office, Cheapside, St Michael, Barbados

BERMUDA
Bermuda is the place for couples who want sunshine and sightseeing but still want the comforts of home. In 1503, Spaniard Juan de Bermudez discovered this beautiful island of turquoise waters and pink-sand beaches. However, Bermuda was not officially colonised until 1612 when the British arrived. The Union Jack has flown here for more than 300 years, and it is the oldest British colony in the Caribbean and the influence is everywhere to see – tidy cottages line the clean streets, and high tea is still served in the island's guesthouses! Many of London's large department stores have branches here, made even more attractive by duty-free prices. A trip to Bermuda encompasses the best of both worlds. After a morning of touring the Royal Naval Dockyard or snorkelling among the coral reefs, you can get married on a beach and then indulge in some of the island's nightlife.

 Star choice
Pop singer Louise and footballer Jamie Redknapp were married on a yacht off Bermuda and then stayed in a villa in the Elbow Beach grounds for their honeymoon. Louise loved the hotel so much she named her next album after it!

Travel time
7 hours.

Waiting period
None specified, but you need 15 days for your notice of intended marriage to clear, although you can submit it before your arrival on the island.

The moongate at the Harmony Club, Bermuda

Documents
- Valid 10-year passports.
- Birth certificates.
- Decree absolute (if divorced).

🦋 DREAM HOTEL
Rosedon Hotel
PO Box HM 290, Hamilton HM AX,
Bermuda
Tel: 00 1 441 295 1640
E-mail:
webmaster@rosedonbermuda.com
Web: www.rosedonbermuda.com

Quiet, friendly and relaxed, Rosedon offers a great wedding package for couples who want the hard work taken out of organising their wedding day. Beach weddings are popular, which you can follow with a romantic cruise or candlelit dinner. The hotel itself makes a lovely honeymoon location too. It has 47 rooms, each one individually decorated and surrounded by lush tropical gardens, plus a great restaurant and a lovely curved beach of golden sand to recline on.

- A notice of intended marriage, which you need to get from the Bermuda Registrar General's office.

Minimum age
21 years. If either of you is under 21, written consent from both parents is needed.

Further information
You must forward a notice of intended marriage (form available from Bermuda Tourism in London, see Contact details) to the Registrar General in Hamilton, Bermuda, together with a bank draft for US $186.80 (£112) plus US $19 (£11) for the certificate, made payable to the Accountant General. Personal cheques are not accepted. The notice of intended marriage must be sent at least two weeks before the marriage is due to take place. Your marriage licence will be issued to you 15 days after your paperwork is received. Once consent is granted you are free to choose where your ceremony is to take place.

Dream hotel
Fairmont Southampton Princess Hotel
PO Box HM 1379
Southampton HM FX, Bermuda
Tel: 00 1 441 238 8000
Web: www.fairmont.com

Perched royally on the island's highest point, the Fairmont Southampton overlooks acres of grounds, pink-sand beaches and lush gardens. Couples can exchange their vows in these tranquil surroundings, and then relax beneath a rainbow of umbrellas at the Beach Club. Other fun things to try while you're there include hitting the links for a round of golf, grabbing a racket for a tennis match, snorkelling your way around the reefs, riding the waves on a jet ski or exploring the island on your scooter. If that's not enough, there's also the luxurious Willow Stream Spa, where you can have a massage before or after the big day, and six restaurants to choose from.

Bermuda has more churches per capita than anywhere else in the world, so a church wedding is a popular choice but it has to be with the consent of the local clergyman. You may also tie the knot in a register office, where the fee is normally US $175 (£105). However, many people go to Bermuda to avoid such formalities, so beaches are the next choice. Outdoor weddings are often conducted under a 'moongate' in Bermuda, which symbolises good luck for the wedding couple and, according to Bermudian tradition, will bring you everlasting happiness if you walk through it!

Weather
May to October are the best months to visit, with constant sunshine and little rainfall.

Contact details
Bermuda Tourism
1 Battersea Church Road, London
SW11 3LY
Tel: 020 7771 7001
Web: www.bermudatourism.com

Registrar General
Government Administration Building,
30 Parliament Street, Hamilton, Bermuda
Tel: 00 1 441 297 7709

For general information
Shelly Hamill (Bermuda wedding organiser)
E-mail: shamill@ibl.bm

Dream hotel
Elbow Beach Hotel
60 South Shore Road, Paget PG 04,
PO Box HM 455, Hamilton HM BX,
Bermuda
Tel: 00 1 441 236 3535
E-mail: ebbda-reservations@mohg.com
Web:
www.mandarinoriental.com/bermuda

In a prime location on Bermuda's South Shore, this pretty hotel, which is part of the Mandarin Oriental Group, sits in 50 acres of botanical gardens. It also overlooks one of the island's most stunning beaches, Elbow Beach, a beautiful expanse of pink sand and the ideal place to exchange your vows. The royal suites are perfect for honeymooners, particularly the Bird of Paradise Cottage, a Bermuda-style villa with private patio and gardens, and so close to the beach you can hear the gentle swish of the waves.

BRITISH VIRGIN ISLANDS

These islands are ideal for lovers – and water-lovers, as they offer some of the best water sports in the world. If you envisaged saying 'I will' beneath a palm tree and then sailing off into the sunset, then this is your place. It's home to the largest fleet of charter yachts in the Caribbean, and is the ideal place to indulge in your favourite water sports or learn new ones. There are relatively few dangerous reefs, with the exception of Anegada, a favourite spot for divers and fishermen, so conditions are ideal even for part-time sailors, with safe waters and a constant breeze to fill your sails. Sparkling sandy bays beneath striking cliffs are favourite stopping-off points for beach picnics, and scuba-diving is popular around sunken reefs and wrecks. Snorkellers should visit the four caves at Norman Island, said to be the setting for Robert Louis Stevenson's *Treasure Island.* Windsurfers benefit from steady winds and calm water. On land, there are national parks to be explored, including Little Fort, with the remains of a Spanish castle, and the Coppermine ruin on Virgin Gorda. For naturalists, Anegada's 1,100-acre bird sanctuary is a must, as is Sage Mountain, the last remnant of a rainforest on Tortola, the BVI's main island.

Travel time

Around 8 hours to Antigua, plus a 30-minute connecting flight to Tortola, the main island, then boat transfer to smaller islands such as Virgin Gorda or Peter Island.

Waiting period

3 working days.

Documents

- Valid 10-year passports (with BVI entry cards).
- Birth certificates.
- Decree absolute (if divorced), death certificate of former spouse (if widowed), deed poll proof (if name changed).

Note: All documents handed to the registrar must be originals or certified copies and in English.

Minimum age

21 years without parental consent. If either of you is under 21, written proof of parental consent is needed.

Further information

The couple to be married must apply in person for a BVI marriage licence at least three working days prior to the ceremony. Applications must be filed at the registrar's office in Tortola, open from Monday to Friday between the hours of 9.00 am and 4.00 pm (except public holidays). The registrar will then confirm the date and time of the ceremony.

The registrar or priest will come to hold the ceremony in a place selected by the couple – usually a resort's beach, terrace or gardens. Two witnesses are needed.

Weather

Temperatures vary very little throughout the year, and are constantly warm, averaging 25°C (76°F). The summer months tend to be a little hotter and wetter than the drier winter months from January to April.

DREAM HOTEL
Peter Island Resort
PO Box 211, Old Town, Tortola, British Virgin Islands
Tel: 00 1 284 494 2561
Web: www.peterisland.com

This is the only resort on this secluded 1,800-acre island with its five beaches, more than 20 coves, and six breathtaking bays. Choose from 52 lovely rooms and suites. Water sports include snorkelling, windsurfing, sailing, and kayaking. Enjoy the pool, fitness centre and spa. Room rates include all meals, and there are three great restaurants and bars to choose from.

Contact details
BVI Tourist Board
15 Upper Grosvenor Street, London
W1K 7PJ
Tel: 020 7355 9585
Web: www.bvigovernment.org

Registrar's Office
PO Box 418, Tortola, British Virgin Islands
Tel: 00 1 284 494 3492
Web: www.bvi.gov.vg

DREAM HOTEL
Biras Creek Resort
Virgin Gorda, British Virgin Islands
Tel: 00 1 800 223 1108
E-mail: caribisles@aol.com
Web: www.biras.com

This 140-acre property with a private beach is accessible only by boat. Choose from 32 rooms and suites. The Arawak Pavilion offers television, a snooker room and a reading den. Enjoy sailing, windsurfing, snorkelling, and kayaking. Play tennis, go hiking, or just relax by the pool. All meals are included in the price and all guests are given a bike to get around the property.

Biras Creek, one of the most romantic resorts in the world, offers couples the perfect wedding in one easily arranged package. The Wedding Package costs US $1,100 (£650) and includes a marriage licence/stamp, registrar's fee, bride's bouquet, wedding cake, champagne and photographer (couples receive three rolls of undeveloped film). A wedding co-ordinator is available on-site to assist with all the arrangements. Other options – such as a video of the proceedings, live music, balloons, wedding arch and hair and beauty services – are available for an additional fee. Couples can choose from a selection of romantic wedding settings including several terraces overlooking the North Sound, the beach at Deep Bay, or in the extensive gardens.

CAYMAN ISLANDS

There are three low-lying islands that make up the Cayman Islands: Grand Cayman, Little Cayman and the wilder, more rugged Cayman Brac. Grand Cayman is the most cosmopolitan of the three, well known for its wealthy citizens and bustling capital, George Town. It is also famous for the gorgeous Seven Mile Beach, one of the Caribbean's most beautiful stretches of sand and the perfect place for a beachside ceremony. If you don't fancy staying in just one place during your honeymoon, it's well worth doing some island-hopping and visiting the other two, less developed isles, where you'll discover deserted beaches and clear turquoise waters and can try snorkelling above the many wrecks caught on the coral reefs that surround the islands.

Travel time
Around 11 hours.

Waiting period
3 working days.

Documents
- Valid 10-year passports.
- Birth certificates.
- Decree absolute (if divorced), marriage certificate and previous spouse's death certificate (if widowed).
- Cayman Islands International embarkation/disembarkation card, provided on arrival.

Minimum age
18 years without parental consent. If either of you is under 18, written proof of parental consent is needed.

Further information
The marriage licence application must give full names, occupations

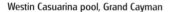

Westin Casuarina pool, Grand Cayman

DREAM HOTEL
Westin Casuarina Resort and Spa

PO Box 30620 SMB, Grand Cayman, Cayman Islands
Tel: 00 1 345 945 3800
E-mail: salesing@candw.ky
Web: www.westincasuarina.com

The Westin Casuarina nestles amongst lush tropical gardens and overlooks 700 feet of the white sands of Seven Mile Beach – a true tropical paradise! There are lots of wedding ceremony and reception locations to choose from, including a 2,600-square-foot ballroom, two executive suites and an open-air function space housing upwards of 450 people. Outdoor venues include a tropical courtyard, which surrounds the largest freshwater pool on Grand Cayman, overlooking the turquoise waters of the Caribbean Sea. Or you could keep it simple and wed on the soft coral sands of Seven Mile Beach itself. When you're relaxing afterwards, take advantage of the fabulous swim-up pool bar, or indulge in some other water-related activities, such as diving, snorkelling, sailing or wave running. The well-appointed bedrooms feature marble baths, balconies, ceiling fans, air conditioning and lots of other extras. Wake up to the sound of the surf and walk barefoot on the beach – the message here is, 'Chill out'.

Dream hotel
Hyatt Regency Grand Cayman

Seven Mile Beach, PO Box 1588 GT, Grand Cayman, Cayman Islands
Tel: 00 1 345 949 1234
E-mail: dunck@camapo.hyatt.com
Web: www.grandcayman.hyatt.com

This hotel is located across from the dazzling Seven Mile Beach, one of the Caymans' most beautiful stretches of sand. If that's not enough to entice you, it's also built for romance, from the courtyards with seats for two, to the tropical gardens and airy bedrooms with champagne on ice. It's large, with 236 rooms, but they are spread out over six buildings, so you won't feel on show. It's a great place to have your wedding, as there are staff on hand to organise everything and help you through the application process. One option to consider is a ceremony on board a catamaran at sunset.

$150 (approximately £120), together with a CI $10 (£7) postage stamp (as stamp duty), must also accompany the above documents. The licence application should be filed at the office of the administrative secretary in George Town (see Contact details). Once it is issued, the licence must be given to the marriage officer performing the ceremony. Couples wishing to be married in the islands are advised to contact one of the civil registrars or marriage officers direct – a full list is available from the Cayman Islands Department of Tourism in London (see Contact details).

All marriages must be attended by a marriage officer and two

and permanent addresses of the bride and the groom and be signed by both. It must also name the marriage officer who is to perform the ceremony, state whether either party has been previously married, and confirm that there is no impediment to the intended marriage. A fee of CI

witnesses. They must take place between the hours of 6.00 am and 8.00 pm, and with the doors to the premises open. In the Cayman Islands, couples have plenty of options for their wedding venue, whether it be in a church, on Seven Mile Beach, on a boat or in a hotel. Pedro St James, a large plantation house restored in 1998, is another popular venue, where you can marry in the house or in the gardens, which look out to the Caribbean Sea.
Note: To be legally binding a civil ceremony must be performed in public.

Weather

The best months to travel to the Cayman Islands are between November and April, as they are the driest months but still very warm.

Contact details

Cayman Islands Department of Tourism
Head Office, The Pavilion Cricket Square, PO Box 67, George Town, Grand Cayman, Cayman Islands
Tel: 00 1 345 949 0623
Web: www.caymanislands.ky

Cayman Islands Department of Tourism
6 Arlington Street, London, SW1A 1RE
Tel: 020 7491 7771
E-mail: info-uk@caymanislands.ky
Web: www.caymanislands.co.uk

Chief Administrative Secretary's Office
4th Floor (Room 406), Government Administration Building, George Town, Grand Cayman, Cayman Islands
Tel: 00 1 345 949 7900
Fax: 00 1 345 949 7544
Web: www.caymans.com

CUBA

This, the largest of the West Indian islands, is rapidly becoming one of the most popular destinations for weddings and honeymoons. With its striking and very varied scenery – wild mountainous areas, tropical forests, beautiful cascading waterfalls and miles and miles of white unspoilt beaches – it's the perfect tropical island escape. Add to this the rich charm of the Spanish colonial heritage in Havana and the nostalgic 1960s' feel of the larger towns, and you have a unique honeymoon experience. And of course we should not forget the island's exciting nightlife, including salsa dancing, which every couple should let their hair down and indulge in during their stay. This is an ideal destination for adventurous couples who want something more than just sun and sand, and it's also an ideal destination to come for a wedding all year round as the weather changes very little from month to month.

Travel time

Around 10 hours.

Waiting period

4 working days.

Documents

- Valid 10-year passports.
- Original birth certificates.
- Decree absolute showing coloured court stamp (if divorced), marriage certificate and previous spouse's death certificate (if widowed), deed poll proof (if name changed), adoption certificate (if adopted).

Dream hotel
Brisas del Caribe
Carretera Punta Hicacos, Varadero, Cuba
Tel: 00 53 239 793 7157
Fax: 00 53 239 775 8300
E-mail: cubanconnection@yahoo.com
Web: www.cuba.tc/CuVarLasBrisas.htm

This is an all-inclusive resort, so you're not going to have to worry about a thing once you've checked in. Even your wedding ceremony will all be taken care of by the resort's friendly staff and whether you want a beachside ceremony or to say 'I will' in the manicured gardens, they've got it covered – all you have to do is turn up.

The hotel lies on a stretch of Varadero Beach, a golden crescent of sand that can get busy but you'll always be able to find a secluded spot just for the two of you. There's also a giant pool to dip your toes into and bedrooms that are simple and tastefully decorated, with king-size beds for you to wallow in.

Minimum age
18 years without parental consent. If either of you is under 18, parental consent is needed in the form of an affidavit stamped by a notary.

Further information
If either of you is divorced or widowed, the documents required must be translated into Spanish before travel (you can inquire at the Cuban Embassy in London about this – it will cost around £30). They must also be certified by a solicitor who must state that they have no reason to doubt the authenticity of the documents. All documents except passports need to be stamped and legalised by the Foreign Office at a cost of £12 per document. They should then be sent to the Cuban Consulate to be legalised at a cost of £88 per document.

Weather
Year-round sunshine, with the hot, rainy season running from May to October.

Contact details
Foreign Office and Commonwealth Office
Old Admiralty Building, Whitehall, London SW1A 2LG
Tel: 020 7008 111
Web: www.fco.gov.uk

Cuban Consulate
167 High Holborn, London WC1 6PA
Tel: 020 7240 2488

 Dream hotel
Hotel Cubanacon Boutique La Unión
Calle 31 esq A 54, Cienfuegos, Cuba
Tel: 00 53 239 793 7157
E-mail: cubanconnection@yahoo.com
Web: www.cuba.tc/La_Union.html

For those who want something a bit more Cuban than a chain hotel, then a trip to the gorgeous La Union is recommended. Situated in downtown Cienfuegos, it's a stunning building with a faded blue and white façade that hides a courtyard with a swimming pool, outdoor jacuzzi and shaded areas to sit and sip coffee while the world goes by. Inside, it's all dark wood furniture, whirring ceiling fans and vast bedrooms with floor-to-ceiling windows. You'll feel like you're in a Graham Greene novel.

DOMINICAN REPUBLIC

The Dominican Republic is part of the lush island of Hispaniola, the second-largest of the Caribbean islands. Its capital, Santa Domingo, is a wonderful place for couples to explore, with its palaces, tree-lined streets and beautiful churches. Inland, it's a stunningly beautiful, very mountainous and heavily forested island, much of which is still very wild and unspoilt. On the coast, there are long stretches of the Caribbean's signature palm-fringed beaches, and the Atlantic Ocean that laps the north side of the island makes it a popular place for water sport lovers, particularly surfers. The towns have a delightfully faded Spanish colonial charm and the hotels and resorts are of a high standard. This is an island for couples who really want to get away from it all and marry somewhere a little bit out of the ordinary.

El Sendero, Dominican Republic

Travel time
10 hours.

Waiting period
3 working days.

Minimum age
18 years without parental consent. If either of you is under 18, parental consent is needed in the form of an affidavit stamped by a notary.

Documents
- Valid 10-year passports.
- Birth certificates.
- Decree absolute (if divorced), former marriage certificate and former spouse's death certificate (if widowed), adoption certificate (if adopted), deed poll proof (if name changed).
- If either of you has not been married before, you will need an affidavit to declare single status.

Further information
Original documents must be sent firstly to the Foreign and Commonwealth Office (see Contact details) to be legalised and then sent to the Dominican Embassy (see Contact details). Costs of legislation are £12 per document at the Foreign and Commonwealth Office and £55 per document at the Dominican Consulate. All documents need to be translated into Spanish, and this can be arranged in most hotels at a cost of around £20 per page of each document.

   You can have a civil or religious ceremony on the island. Civil ceremonies can be performed anywhere, such as on the beach or in hotel gardens. All you need are the documents listed above. For a religious ceremony, there are a few things to bear in mind. Roman Catholic ceremonies are performed in Spanish only (no translator may be used). Original documents as follows must be submitted to your chosen church upon your arrival: valid passport; birth certificate; baptism certificate; confirmation certificate; if widowed, your previous spouse's death certificate; a release from your church authorising the marriage in the Dominican Republic; and a prenuptial certificate indicating you have received instructions from the church.

Note: Marriage records in the Dominican Republic are kept for only two years, so it is important to make copies immediately of your wedding certificates.

Weather

Consistent sunshine but the best months with the least rainfall run from November to April. Wettest months are July to October.

Contact details

Dominican Republic Tourist Board
18–21 Hand Court, High Holborn, London
WC1V 6JF
Tel: 020 7242 7778
E-mail: greatbritain@sectur.gov.do
Web: www.dominicana.com

Embassy of the Dominican Republic
139 Inverness Terrace, Bayswater, London
W2 6JF
Tel: 020 7727 6214

Foreign and Commonwealth Office
The Old Admiralty Building, Whitehall,
London SW1A 2LG
Tel: 020 7008 1111
Web.www.fco.gov.uk

 DREAM HOTEL
Casa de Campo
PO Box 140 La Romana, Dominican
Republic
Tel: 00 1 809 523 3333
E-mail: casadecampo@codetel.com.do
Web: www.casadecampo.cc

This vast, luxury resort sits in 7,000 tropical acres, so you're not going to be short of romantic places to wed. It's actually got a Roman Catholic church on the property, so is the ideal place for a religious ceremony to begin your life together. If you're not of the Roman Catholic faith, you can exchange your vows on the steps of the church or at any other location in the resort's grounds, including a decorated wedding gazebo, and the sandy beach is always a popular choice. Whatever you choose, experienced wedding co-ordinators are on hand to help you with all the details from start to finish.

 DREAM HOTEL
Breezes Puerto Plata
Dominican Republic
Tel: 00 1 809 925 0925 and 0877 467 8737
E-mail: info@superclubs.com
Web: www.superclubs.com

A large, buzzy hotel that has 466 guest rooms and suites surrounded by a tropical garden of 62 acres and overlooking a lovely sandy bay, the wedding ceremony is complimentary if you stay for three nights or more. It's got all the luxuries you'd want for a week of romantic bliss: all the bedrooms are equipped with CD player to play your favourite tunes, king-size beds and a balcony or terrace to watch the sunset.

GRENADA

Grenada, or the Spice Island as it's otherwise known, is one of the Windward Isles and a favourite of British tourists. It's incredibly

> 🏹 DREAM HOTEL
> **Spice Island Beach Resort**
> Grand Anse Beach, PO Box 6,
> St George's, Grenada, West Indies
> Tel: 00 1 473 444 4258/4423/4789
> E-mail: spiceisl@caribsurf.com
> Web: www.spicebeachresort.com
>
> Situated on a secluded stretch of the glorious Grand Anse, which is consistently voted one of the Caribbean's best beaches, the Spice Island Beach Resort is one of the finest hotels on the island. You can marry at the resort, most couples choosing to say 'I will' on the beach, and there is a free honeymoon package of Swedish massage, sunset cruise, fruit, sparkling wine and room upgrade if available. It makes an ideal honeymoon spot too: dotted around the lush tropical flora of the landscaped grounds are 66 rooms, including airy beach-front bungalows with whirlpool baths, and stunning private pool suites, all with spacious patios or balconies. The main building houses the beautiful Sea and Surf Lounge, ideal for pre-dinner cocktails, and Oliver's Restaurant, which specialises in creole and international cuisine. There's also a large swimming pool to lounge around. Health and fitness fanatics will want to make use of the water sports, which include snorkelling and windsurfing, and the floodlit tennis courts, before relaxing in the state-of-the-art spa that provides therapeutic massages and treatments using local products.

picturesque, particularly St George's, the capital, a brightly coloured cluster of buildings overlooking a pretty harbour. Here you can shop in the market for souvenirs, sample the local rum and smell the delicious spices, such as nutmeg, cloves and vanilla. Romantics will take delight in walking barefoot hand-in-hand along its 45 beaches, considered some of the best in the Caribbean. Other attractions include hiking in the rainforest, bathing beneath waterfalls and snorkelling above the coral reefs.

Travel time
Just under 10 hours.

Waiting period
3 working days.

Documents
- Valid 10-year passports.
- Birth certificates.
- Decree absolute (if divorced), marriage certificate and previous spouse's death certificate (if widowed), adoption certificate (if adopted), deed poll proof (if name changed).
- Statutory declaration of single status from a solicitor, or a letter from a clergyman, lawyer or registrar on official letterhead, to attest that you're single and free to marry.

Minimum age
21 years without parental consent. If either of you is aged under 21 years, proof of parental consent is required in the form of an affidavit, stamped and signed by a solicitor.

Further information

Licence and stamp duty fees and copies of marriage certificate will cost EC $35 (£23). You can make an application for a licence at the Prime Minister's office (see below) after the necessary stamp duty and licence fees have been paid. This process takes approximately two days, but slightly longer if either of you is divorced, as your documents must then be sent to the Ministry of Legal Affairs.

In Grenada, you can be married in a civil ceremony by a magistrate or in a church ceremony by a minister – the choice is yours, as is the location. Popular choices are the pretty local chapels, beaches or simply in the grounds of your hotel.

Weather

January to April is the driest time, with average temperatures above 27°C (81°F). It's hotter and more humid during the rest of the year.

Contact details

Grenada Board of Tourism
1 Collingham Gardens, Earl's Court, London SW5 0HW
Tel: 020 7771 7016
E-mail: grenada@compuserve.com
Web: www.grenada.org

Office of the Prime Minister
Ministerial Complex, Tanteen, St George's, Grenada, West Indies
Tel: 00 1 473 440 2255
E-mail: gndpm@caribsurf.com

DREAM HOTEL
Calabash Hotel
L'Anse aux Epines, PO Box 382, St George's, Grenada, West Indies
Tel: 00 1 473 444 4334
E-mail: calabash@caribsurf.com
Web: www.calabashhotel.com

With its eight acres of landscaped gardens overlooking tranquil Prickly Bay, this is a popular spot for ceremonies. Weddings are planned individually, and there's no danger of bumping into another bride and groom on your wedding day as there would never be more than one ceremony allowed on the same day. Couples adore the Calabash for its privacy: there are only 30 luxury suites, eight with private plunge pools and 22 with whirlpools. It's also developed a reputation for its restaurant where celeb chef Gary Rhodes is an adviser. But best of all for newlyweds who want to hide away are the breakfasts, which are cooked and served on your own private patio.

Ministry of Legal Affairs
Church Street, St George's, Grenada, West Indies
Tel: 00 1 473 440 2050

Grenada High Commission
5 Chandos Street, London W1G 9DG
Tel: 020 7631 4277

Dunns River Falls, Jamaica

JAMAICA

The third-largest of the Caribbean islands is the most well known in the UK and a very popular place to tie the knot. Those who travel there for the first time always express their delight because, while Jamaica has the same golden beaches and palms as the rest of the islands, it can also boast an interior that's just as beautiful. The Blue Mountains, home of the world's finest coffee bean, are spectacular, the snaking rivers and crashing waterfalls, such as famous Dunn's River Falls, are captivating and the music, food and drinks that you'll find in the colourful villages and towns around this isle are second to none.

Travel time
10 hours to Montego Bay.

Waiting period
2 working days.

Documents
- Valid 10-year passports.
- Birth certificates.
- Decree absolute (if divorced), marriage certificate and previous spouse's death certificate (if widowed), adoption certificate (if adopted), deed poll proof (if name changed).

Minimum age
21 years without parental consent. If either of you is under 21, proof of parental consent is required in the form of an affidavit stamped by a notary.

Further information
If either of you has never been married, you will need to take an affidavit declaring your single status. All copies of documents need to be stamped and signed in red or blue ink by a notary.

JAMAICA

Weather

It's very hot all year round, with temperatures averaging 31°C (88°F), the driest months being December to April, and the wettest May to October.

Contact details

Jamaica Tourist Board
1–2 Prince Consort Road, London SW7 2BZ
Tel: 020 7224 0505
E-mail: jamaicatravel@btconnect.com
Web: www.jamaicatravel.com

Ministry of National Security and Justice
12 Ocean Boulevard, Kingston, Jamaica, West Indies
Tel: 00 1 876 922 0080
Web: www.weddingsinjamaica.com

DREAM HOTEL
Half Moon Golf, Tennis and Beach Club
PO Box 80, Montego Bay, Jamaica
Tel: 00 1 876 953 2211
E-mail: hmoonres@infochan.com
Web: www.halfmoon-resort.com

A vast 400-acre resort set on a peninsula with its own mile-long crescent of white-sand beach. Lots of famous faces have walked though the doors, including Sean Connery, Whitney Houston and even Prince Charles. It's very popular for weddings because of the pretty gazebo set at the end of a long jetty out to sea – there's no better place to get married as the sun sets. Accommodation is as luxurious as you'd expect: the brilliant white villas have vast king-size beds and French doors that open on to private balconies, and some have private pools and gardens. The resort has three outstanding restaurants, a spa and lots of sports facilities.

DREAM HOTEL
Ritz-Carlton Golf and Spa Resort
Rose Hall, PO Box 1038, Jamaica, West Indies
Tel: 00 1 876 518 0100

This lovely resort sits in 5,000 lush acres overlooking a beautiful palm-fringed, golden beach in the Rose Hall area of Montego Bay, north-west Jamaica, with the Donald Sangster Airport just a 15-minute limousine ride away. There are four wedding packages to choose from and lots of locations, including a lovely wedding pavilion situated in a secluded section of the resort overlooking a quiet stretch of golden beach. You can even arrange to get an outdoor massage in the pavilion if you're feeling stressed before the big day! There's a wedding concierge to take care of all arrangements from the flowers to the marriage licence. The hotel itself is an exquisitely designed five-star retreat of palatial proportions. The decor is classically elegant – think dark wood furniture, dazzling chandeliers, neutral walls and expensive fabrics. There are 427 ultra-stylish rooms that are temples to comfort and minimalist simplicity; huge beds with crisp white sheets and goose-down pillows, marble bathrooms, private balconies and well-stocked mini-bars – and if you ask for the romance option, they'll fill it with passion fruit juice and chocolate kisses!

Montego Bay, Jamaica

MARGARITA

Its distinctly Latin American feel makes this pretty island stand out from other Caribbean destinations. It's not a hugely popular destination for British tourists to marry, but who wants to follow the crowd? It's got lots of appeal, particularly the beautiful beaches, some of which are almost as wild and untouched as they were a century ago. Yet there are lots of towns and villages to explore too, where you'll find bars and restaurants to sample and get a chance to meet the friendly islanders.

Travel time
Around 9 hours 30 minutes.

Waiting period
3 working days.

Documents
- Valid 10-year passports.
- Birth certificates.
- Decree absolute (if divorced), marriage certificate and previous spouse's death certificate (if widowed), adoption certificate (if adopted), deed poll proof (if name changed).

Minimum age
18 years without parental consent. If either of you is under 18, proof of parental consent in the form of an affidavit is required, stamped and signed by a solicitor.

Further information
A single statutory declaration per person, not per couple, must be signed and stamped by a solicitor and the wording should state 'solicitor' clearly on the document. The declaration must be issued within three months of the intended marriage date.

The ceremony must be performed in the local language (Spanish) and the marriage certificate is also issued in Spanish – this can be translated on return to the UK for around £25.

Weather
It's very hot all year, the driest months being December to April, and the wettest May to October

Contact details
Venezuelan Embassy
1 Cromwell Road, London SW7 2HW
Tel: 020 7584 4206

 DREAM HOTEL
**Hesperia Isla Margarita
Golf, Spa and Beach Resort**
Margarita
Tel: 00 58 295 416 7145
Fax: 00 58 295 262 7419
E-mail:
info@hesperiaislamargarita.com
Web: www.hesperiaislamargarita.com

Facing the turquoise sea and a pristine strip of beach, this five-star resort is considered one of the best hotels on the island. It is used to arranging weddings, and can help you through the process of obtaining your licence. Whichever spot you choose to exchange vows will be decorated on the big day, and the hotel also treats you to a candlelit dinner on your wedding night. Accommodation is pretty impressive: there are 312 spacious deluxe rooms, including 17 suites, which have lots of extras such as comfy lounge areas and wraparound sea-view balconies.

🏹 DREAM HOTEL
Dunes Beach Resort
Valle Pedro Gonzalez, Sector El
Pueblito, Juan Griego, Margarita
Tel: 00 95 631333

L ocated on the north end of the island, overlooking the divine Puerto Cruz beach, the hotel is a nature-lover's paradise. It's surrounded by mountains and sea and has gardens full of mangroves, beach grape tree and fragrant hibiscus. Romantics will love the lighthouse in the resort's ground, which offers a spectacular view of the coast and adjacent bays. It's a great place to watch the sun rise or set, and both will make an unusual feature in your wedding photographs. Weddings here are organised by a co-ordinator, so all you have to do is sit back and get a tan. The resort's Mediterranean architecture together with its tropical decor of rattan and light wood is an ideal combination to make a stunning Caribbean hideaway.

MARTINIQUE

This island has a reputation for being very exclusive, and it's easy to see why. It's long been a popular retreat for the rich and famous and its strong links with France means it's often seen as a truly chic destination. The capital, Fort-de-France, is a waterfront town that has lots of great restaurants and bars, while inland you can enjoy dramatic scenery of lush rainforests and soaring mountains. The beaches are high quality but can get busy. It's a wonderful place to head for if you're looking for a destination with a little bit of glitz and glamour for your wedding.

Travel time
Around 10 hours.

Waiting period
One of you must have been resident on the island for at least 1 month.

Documents
- Birth certificates (original or copy with raised seal).
- Certificate of good conduct.
- Certification of single status.
- Residency card.

Minimum age
18 years without parental consent.

Further information
You'll each need a medical certificate, including blood test, issued within three months of the marriage, and a French translation of your English documents. A *bulletin de mariage* (marriage certificate) will be given to you at the ceremony. No fee is involved.

Weather

Hottest from May to October but that's also the wettest period. The best time to go for ideal temperatures and few showers is January to April.

Contact details

French Government Tourist Office
178 Piccadilly, London W1J 9AL
Tel: 09068 244123

DREAM HOTEL
Habitation Lagrange

Le Marigot, 97225, Martinique
Tel: 00 596 53 60 60
Web: www.habitation-lagrange.com

A fairy-tale hotel full of colonial charm located in the pretty village of Marigot on the Atlantic Coast. It's small – there are just 15 rooms – but perfectly formed. Everywhere you tread, there's something to marvel at, from the mahogany rocking chairs and writing desks in the lounge to the eighteenth-century fresco in the dining room. Ask for the first floor suite in the main house, which has a wedding chamber, lounge and circular balcony.

PUERTO RICO

From some of the Caribbean's most exciting nightlife to breathtaking natural wonders, world-class shopping and great beaches, the vibrant island of Puerto Rico is a must for couples who want entertainment as well as sunshine and sand on their trip of a lifetime. Lovers of culture and cuisine will want to explore historic Old San Juan and the distinctive blend of old and new that makes for Puerto Rico's diverse culinary offerings. For sun-worshippers who just want to lie on the sand and soak up the Caribbean rays, Puerto Rico has miles and miles of pristine beaches. Those who are more actively inclined can indulge in water sports, scuba-dive in some of the best locations in the world, marvel at fascinating natural wonders or play golf on one of the island's championship links. And at night, you can dance to the exciting beat of Puerto Rican salsa or enjoy the casinos, discos and nightclubs.

Travel time

Around 8 hours.

Bay of Fort de France, Martinique

Traditional 'Plena' dance, Puerto Rico

 DREAM HOTEL
Ritz-Carlton San Juan Hotel, Spa and Casino
6961 Avenue of the Governors, Isla Verde, Carolina, Puerto Rico, 00979 United States of America
Tel: 00 1 787 253 1700
Web: www.ritzcarlton.com

For the picture-perfect blend of serene tropical beauty and high-rolling excitement, look no further than this extremely luxurious 414-room hotel. It's a really James Bond-type setting for your wedding, with sparkling swimming pools, beachside bars and a casino where you can have a flutter on the roulette wheel if you're feeling lucky after you've made your vows! There's also a perfect golden-sand beach, water sports and a really great spa offering body and beauty treatments. If you need even more to entertain you, it's just minutes from historic San Juan and its exciting nightlife.

Waiting period
As long as it takes to complete the licence requirements (see below).

Documents
- Valid 10-year passports.
- Birth certificates.
- Decree absolute with raised seal (if divorced).
- A declaration certifying that you're not already married, sworn before a notary or other authorised person.

All documents have to be authenticated at the marriage licence bureau.

Minimum age
18 years without parental consent. With parents' consent, 16- to 17-year-olds may also marry.

Further information
The couple must both appear in person at the time of collecting the licence, but can apply for it first in

writing (see Contact details). All applications must be accompanied by copies of the documents listed above. There is no fee for the licence, but private or hotel fees for a ceremony usually cost US $150–350 (£90–210). Once granted, the licence is good indefinitely but can only be used within the United States or Puerto Rico. Marriages may be performed by a judge in his chambers or in open court at no fee. They may also be performed by any clergyman authorised to perform marriage ceremonies.

Weather

January to May are the driest months to visit; from June to October it's hotter but expect more rainfall.

Contact details

Puerto Rico Tourism Company
2nd Floor, 67a High Street,
Walton-on-Thames, Surrey KT12 1DJ
Tel: 01932 253302
E-mail: PuertoRicoUK@aol.com
Web: www.GotoPuertoRico.com

For copies of your certificate of marriage

Department of Health
Demographic Registry, PO Box 11854,
Fernandez Juncos Station, San Juan,
Puerto Rico 00910
Tel: 00 1 787 728 7980

For marriage licence papers

Demographic Registry
PO Box 11854, Fernandez Juncos Station,
San Juan, Puerto Rico 00910
Tel: 00 1 787 728 7980
(Apply in writing and allow 2 months)

DREAM HOTEL
Wyndham El Conquistador Resort

51000 Conquistador Avenue, Fajardo
00738, Puerto Rico
Tel: 00 1 787 863 1000
Web: www.wyndham.com

This huge resort has quite simply everything you could need for a laid-back wedding and honeymoon. Lots of prime locations for you to say 'I will', including a beach and gazebo in the gardens, a private marina, beaches, the Golden Door spa and even the shops. It's the ideal place to head if you simply want to chill out together and not have to move a muscle – apart from indulging in all the water sports and trying one of the 16 restaurants! There's even a choice of accommodation. The Grand Hotel rises above it all with panoramic views, spacious bathrooms and walk-in closets. The ultra-luxurious Las Casitas Village offers a Spanish-style atmosphere with private check-in, pool and personal butler. The villas of Las Olas Village are built into the side of a cliff and offer breathtaking ocean views, while the balconies of La Marina Village overlook the sea – just steps from the marina and quaint shops.

ST BARTHELEMY

There's something about the French West Indies that has a shade of glitz and glamour that's hard to define, and St Barthelemy – or St Barts – has more than most. Maybe it's something to do with all the rich sophisticates that have villas there – the Rockefellers, Rothschilds and Fords, to name but a few. It's often referred to as the St Tropez of the Caribbean, which should give you a good indication as to whether it's the right sort of destination for you. It's not the most beautiful of islands in the Caribbean, so don't head here to wed if you want lots of flora and fauna, but if you're foodies who enjoy people-watching and hanging out on cool beaches and bars, then this is your dream destination.

 DREAM HOTEL
Hotel Le Toiny

Anse de Toiny – F, St Barthelemy, French West Indies
Tel: 00 1 590 29 77 50
E-mail: letoiny@saint-barths.com
Web: www.letoiny.com

A seriously romantic hotel that sits on a bay overlooking a lagoon and the open sea, so there's water as far as the eye can see. It's also seriously luxurious: each of the 13 suites has its own private pool, terrace with chaises longues and a four-poster mahogany bed. The main building is like a comfortable colonial house, and houses a bar, lounge and restaurant. It's made for honeymooners and is an ideal size to take over if you've got a big budget and want to have a wedding celebration with family and friends.

 DREAM HOTEL
Guanahani

Anse de Grand Cul de Sac, St Barthelemy, French West Indies
Tel: 00 1 590 276660
E-mail: guanahani@wanadoo.fr
Web: www.leguanahani.com

A truly outstanding hotel that manages to be extremely luxurious while maintaining lots of French Caribbean charm. Its chic, colourful bungalow-style cottages, painted in fun hues of yellow, indigo, purple and green, are delightful. Inside, they're all furnished in cotton fabrics, polished wood and pretty pastel shades for a calm, relaxing vibe. There's a glorious sandy beach protected by a reef, and the hotel sits above it on a small headland so the rooms have great panoramic views of the sea. A really special retreat for newlyweds.

Travel time
Around 8 hours to Antigua, then a 35-minute connecting flight to St Barts.

Waiting period
One partner must have been resident on the island for at least 1 month.

Documents
- Valid 10-year passports.
- Birth certificates (original or copy with raised seal).
- Certificate of good conduct.
- Certification of single status.
- Residency card, given out when you enter the country.

Minimum age
18 years without parental consent.

A pool with a view, the Carl Gustav Hotel, St Barthelemy

Further information

You will need a medical certificate (including a blood test), issued within three months of marriage, and a French translation of all English documents. A *bulletin de mariage* (marriage certificate) will be given to you at the ceremony. No fee is involved.

Weather

Hot and sunny most of the year, but the driest period runs from December to April.

Contact details

French Government Tourist Office
178 Piccadilly, London W1J 9AL
Tel: 09068 244123

ST KITTS AND NEVIS

St Kitts is a very scenic island, dominated by the dormant volcano of Mount Liamuiga towering over the sugar cane plantations, forests and beaches. It's a quiet, laid-back island so a good destination for couples looking to flop on a sunlounger and soak up the sun straight after their wedding! The tiny island of Nevis, just a couple of miles to the south of St Kitts, is even more tranquil and well known as one of the Caribbean's more exclusive destinations. There are several boutique retreats here and some great restaurants.

Travel time

8 hours to St Kitts. Onward flights to Nevis are available but it is more usual to fly to Antigua (8 hours) and take a 30-minute connecting flight.

Waiting period

One of you must be resident on the islands for 2 working days prior to your marriage. See also Further information, below.

Documents

- Valid 10-year passports.
- Birth certificates.
- Decree absolute (if divorced), marriage and previous spouse's death certificate (if widowed), deed poll proof (if name changed), adoption certificate (if adopted).

DREAM HOTEL
Montpelier Plantation
PO Box 474, Nevis, West Indies
Tel: 001 869 469 3462
E-mail: info@montpeliernevis.com

The Montpelier is a former sugar plantation restored with impeccable taste, with 17 cottage-style rooms nestling in flower-filled gardens with private verandas looking out to sea. It's the sort of place where time stands still and you can get in some proper relaxation, so it's an ideal place if you want a laid-back wedding and honeymoon. Weddings are customised to suit the unique desires of each couple. There are lots of pretty venues to choose from – the gardens, on the beach or in the old sugar mill that stands in the grounds. The staff will take care of all the legal arrangements, and there are lots of other luxuries on offer. Bedrooms have a choice of either four-poster or canopy bed, you can book massages for two in the room or on the beach, and a special candlelit dinner can be arranged in the Mill Restaurant or on the terrace.

Ottley's Plantation Inn, St Kitts

Minimum age

18 years without parental consent. If either of you is under 18, parental consent in the form of a statutory declaration, stamped and signed by a solicitor, must be provided.

Further information

There are two types of marriage licence that are available on the islands. The ordinary licence, costing EC $50 (£35), dictates that one of you has to be resident in St Kitts or Nevis for 15 days preceding the date of the application for the licence. The special licence, costing EC $200 (£160), specifies that one of you has to be resident in St Kitts or Nevis for two working days prior to the date of your wedding. Application forms for either licence must be obtained from the legal department on the islands (see below). Payment is made in the form of stamp duty and the stamps can be purchased at the Post Office, Bay Road, Basseterre, St Kitts, and at the Post Office, Main Street, Charlestown, Nevis. The application forms must be completed and signed in the presence of a Justice of Peace and the cost for their services varies between EC $30 (£20) and EC $50 (£30). The completed forms must then be returned to the legal department. The whole process takes around two working days.

If a Roman Catholic minister is to perform the ceremony, a letter from your parish priest must be produced verifying that you are free to marry and that you have received the necessary instructions. Your ceremony can be held in the grounds of your hotel, in a church of almost any denomination, amongst historic ruins, in a rustic gazebo in a picturesque garden and, of course, on the beach.

Weather

December to April is the best time to visit, with high temperatures and low rainfall.

Contact details

St Kitts and Nevis Tourist Office
10 Kensington Court, London W8 5DL
Tel: 020 7376 0881
E-mail: uk-europe.office@stkittstourism.kn
Web: interknowledge.com/stkitts-nevis

Government Headquarters
Church Street, Basseterre, St Kitts,
West Indies
Tel: 00 1 869 465 2521

Legal Office
Government Road, Charlestown, Nevis,
West Indies
Tel: 00 1 869 469 5521

DREAM HOTEL
Ottley's Plantation Inn
PO Box 345, St Kitts, West Indies
Tel: 00 1 869 465 7234/4760
E-mail: ottleys@caribsurf.com
Web: www.ottleys.com

Situated on 35 acres of rolling lawns and gardens at the foot of majestic Mt Liamuiga, with breathtaking views of the Atlantic, Ottley's is a magnificent Caribbean hideaway. The attractive yellow and white building dates back to the eighteenth century and there's a wrap around veranda where you can sit and gaze out at the beautiful gardens, making this an ideal spot for a low-key wedding in glorious surroundings. Wedding packages are available or you can tailor-make your own.

ST LUCIA

The dominating features of this lush isle are the twin mountain peaks of Les Deux Pitons rising out of the sea in the south of the island. It's also renowned for its active volcano – you can drive right up to it and bathe in the sulphur springs – dense rainforest, which carpets much of the land, pretty fishing villages and great beaches. It's a laid-back place, but there are pockets of nightlife, such as Gros Islet, which has a giant street party every Friday night where couples can enjoy the sounds of reggae and sample jerk chicken. It's an ideal place for brides and grooms looking for a relaxing destination with plenty of activities and entertainment too.

 DREAM HOTEL
Anse Chastanet
PO Box 7000, Soufriere, St Lucia, West Indies
Tel: 00 1 758 459 7000
E-mail: ansechastanet@candw.lc
Web: www.ansechastanet.com

Ideal for romantic couples who want somewhere off the beaten track, this pretty boutique hotel sits in a 600-acre estate, and is very secluded and private. Weddings are a unique affair here: every ceremony is organised in personal consultation with the bride and groom who can also add their own vows to the civil ceremony. There is no dedicated wedding chapel; instead the bride and groom choose their own very special location, be it the Treehouse, the beach, an old colonial plantation, a nearby waterfall, the coral reef or the privacy of their room. Honeymooners staying seven nights or more receive a bottle of champagne and one-hour spa treatment. The 49 rooms don't have telephones or televisions, but they do offer fabulous views of the ocean and famous Piton mountain peaks. A word of warning though: this isn't a good place for people who have problems walking long distances, as there are 100 steps down to the beach from the hillside rooms.

Travel time
Around 8 hours 30 minutes.

Waiting period
4 working days.

Documents
- Valid 10-year passports.
- Birth certificates.
- Decree absolute (if divorced), marriage certificate and previous spouse's death certificate (if widowed), adoption certificate (if adopted), deed poll proof (if name changed).

Minimum age
18 years without parental consent. If either of you is under 18, proof of parental consent is needed in the form of a sworn affidavit stamped by a notary.

Further information
Once you've been on the island for two days you can apply for a marriage licence, which must be obtained two days before the wedding, at a cost of EC $102.50 (£60).

Weather
Average year-round temperature of 26°C (80°F). The best months to visit are January to June. Tropical showers are likely at any time and the wettest months are from July to November.

 DREAM HOTEL
Windjammer Landing Villa Beach Resort
Labrelotte Bay, PO Box 1504, Castries, St Lucia, West Indies
Tel: 00 1 758 456 9000
E-mail: reservations@windjammer-landing.com
Web: www.windjammer-landing.com

Nestling in a hillside above Labrelotte Bay sits this charming village-like hotel. There are free wedding packages available to couples staying six nights and honeymooners staying seven nights or more receive sparkling wine, fruit and a free half-hour massage. The 237 rooms are in whitewashed villas with picturesque arched windows and red tiled roofs. The main house sits overlooking the bay, where there are three restaurants, a giant swimming pool and lots of water sports to indulge in. You can zip around the resort in golf buggies, so you won't get tired walking back up the hillside after your sundowner cocktail.

Contact details
St Lucia Tourist Board
1 Collingham Gardens, London SW5 0HW
Tel: 0870 900 7697
E-mail: sltbinfo@stluciauk.org

Les Deux Pitons, St Lucia

ST VINCENT AND THE GRENADINES

This archipelago of 32 tiny islands in the Eastern Caribbean runs from St Vincent in the north down to Palm Island in the south and they are extremely popular with yachtsmen and those seeking the ultimate peaceful, tranquil retreat. The islands and cays offer everything romantic couples need for a wedding in the sun – white coral-sand beaches lapped by crystal-clear waters and lots of swaying palms. The main island is St Vincent, which is the largest at 18 miles long and 11 miles wide; other gems are Mustique and Union and Palm Islands.

 DREAM HOTEL
The Cotton House Resort
Mustique
Tel: 0800 894 057
E-mail: CaribIsles@aol.com
Web: www.cottonhouseresort.com

The Cotton House Resort is located on Mustique, a private island estate near St Vincent. Surrounded by the Caribbean Sea to the west and the Atlantic Ocean to the east, it's one of the most idyllic wedding locations in the world. Choosing exactly where to hold your ceremony is the only problem you'll have here, but luckily there are staff on hand to help you decide as you stroll round the grounds. They'll also help you with other details of the big day, from introducing you to the officiating minister to travelling with you to obtain your marriage licence in St Vincent. Included in a basic wedding package are a cake, champagne for the toast and reception with a selection of hot and cold appetisers. There is also the option of an evening sunset cruise with canapés and cocktails. You'll find it's a charming place to spend your honeymoon too, with accommodation in pretty cottages and houses hidden in the beautifully landscaped gardens rising up from glorious L'Ansecoy Bay. An old sugar mill, remnant of a bygone era, still stands in the grounds and is a popular feature in wedding photographs.

Travel time
No direct flights available. 8 hours to Barbados, then an average 50-minute connecting flight to the islands.

Bequia, St Vincent and the Grenadines

Waiting period
3 days.

Documents
- Valid 10-year passports.
- Birth certificates.
- Decree absolute (if divorced), marriage certificate and previous spouse's death certificate (if widowed), adoption certificate (if adopted), deed poll proof (if name changed).

Minimum age
18 years without parental consent.

Further information
An application for a marriage licence can't be made in advance by mail. Instead, you have to apply in person at the Ministry of Justice in St Vincent (see Contact details); the application can be processed in around two hours. The registrar's licence application costs around EC $5 (£3), the licence itself EC $35 (£20).

Weather
It's driest December to May, with rainfall heavier between June and November. Hot and sunny all year round.

Contact details
Ministry of Justice
Egmont Street, Kingstown, St Vincent and the Grenadines
Tel: 00 1 809 457 1648

 Star choice
TV presenter and model Melanie Sykes and her boyfriend Daniel Caltagirone were a recent celebrity couple to fly out to Mustique for an intimate exchange of vows.

 DREAM HOTEL
Palm Island Resort
Palm Island, St Vincent and the Grenadines
Tel: 0870 160 9645
Web: www.palmislandresorts.com

Situated in the island chain of St Vincent and the Grenadines, Palm Island is located on its own private 135-acre island hideaway at the end of the Windward Island group of the Eastern Caribbean. This little haven is accessible via a ten-minute ride aboard the resort's launch from Union Island, a journey that you'll find fun and refreshing after a long flight. When you arrive, you'll fall instantly in love with the lush tropical landscapes embraced by five dazzling white-sand beaches. Sumptuous gourmet dining served on the oceanfront by award-winning chefs makes for an incredibly romantic setting. All 40 intimate guest rooms are air-conditioned and feature traditional handmade rattan furnishings and plenty of extras to pamper you, such as fluffy bathrobes and lots of toiletries, and the vantage-point from your private balcony or patio provides a sweeping panoramic view of the coast. Weddings here are pretty special too – it's up to you whether you say 'I will' on one of the beaches, in the grounds or on your own private terrace.

St Vincent and the Grenadines Tourist Office
10 Kensington Court, London W8 5DL
Tel: 020 7937 6570
Web: www.svgtourism.com

TOBAGO

Usually paired with Trinidad, this is the smaller, quieter island of the two, but it is by no means any less special. It's very much a picture-postcard Caribbean destination, with a fabulous easy-going atmosphere and plenty of white-sand, palm-fringed beaches, as well as traditional, colourful fishing villages such as Castara and Parlatuvier in the north-east of the island. Like many of the Windward Islands, it's well known for its lush vegetation and rainforest interior, due to the bursts of heavy rain that may occur from June to December. It's also one of the best places in the Caribbean to indulge in scuba-diving and snorkelling.

Travel time
Just under 9 hours.

Waiting period
3 working days.

Documents
- Valid 10-year passports.
- Birth certificates.
- Decree absolute (if divorced), marriage certificate and previous spouse's death certificate (if widowed), adoption certificate (if adopted), deed poll proof (if name changed).
- Affidavit to prove single status.

Minimum age
18 years without parental consent.

Further information
You need to contact the Warden's office, open 8.30 am to 4.00 pm from Monday to Friday, or the Registrar General's office (see Contact details). Both parties must

attend one of the offices no less than 24 hours before the intended time of marriage in order to make an affidavit or statutory declaration and to pay a fee of TT $ 337.50 (£33)for the licence fee. You must take all the necessary documents listed above.

No ceremony can be performed after 6.00 pm in the evening. Popular locations include hotel grounds, beaches, rainforests or the Fort King George set on a hillside above Scarborough, the capital city. Ceremonies are conducted by a local minister, justice of the peace or registrar.

 DREAM HOTEL
Coco Reef Resort and Spa
PO Box 434, Scarborough, Tobago, West Indies
Tel: 00 1 868 639 8571
E-mail: cocoreef-tobago@trinidad.net
Web: www.cocoreef.com

It's often cited as the best hotel on the island, and one of the best in the Caribbean, and for good reason. It sits on the white-sand stretch of Coconut Beach, and is thoroughly Caribbean in decor and spirit. The impressive lobby, which has 30-foot palm trees growing in it, has stunning views of the shore and a grand staircase leads from it to the relaxed Gallery Bar. Throughout the grounds there are splashes of colour from bougainvillaea and hibiscus, and the rooms are splendid, packed with hand-crafted wicker furniture and spacious balconies. There are enticing wedding packages here, including offers of free weddings for couples staying a minimum of 14 nights.

Weather

Average year-round temperature of 30°C (86°F). The best months to visit are December through to March.

Contact details

Trinidad and Tobago Tourism Office
Mitre House, 66 Abbey Road, Bush Hill Park, Enfield, Middlesex EN1 2QE
Tel: 020 8350 1009

Warden's Office
TIDCO Mall, Scarborough, Tobago, West Indies
Tel: 00 1 868 639 2410

Registrar General's Office
Jeminingham Street, Scarborough, Tobago, West Indies
Tel: 00 1 868 639 3210
Web: www.tobagoweddings.com

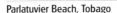

DREAM HOTEL
Blue Haven

c/o Robinson Crusoe Beach Resort Ltd, Bacolet Bay, Scarborough, Tobago, West Indies
Tel: 00 1 868 660 7400/7500/7600
E-mail: info@bluehavenhotel.com
Web: www.bluehavenhotel.com

A favourite of Hollywood stars in the 1950s, this is a little gem of a hotel that was totally refurbished in 2000. The result is pretty spectacular. The buildings are painted in an array of colourful pinks, blues and yellows and the gourmet restaurant, Shutters on the Bay, is housed in a colonial-style villa. The elements that first attracted the stars are still here, however, including the secluded beach, vast pool, and spacious rooms that all have balcony or patio with great views of the sea. A great place to say 'I will'.

Parlatuvier Beach, Tobago

Mardi Gras, Trinidad

TRINIDAD

Trinidad is a buzzy, lively island famed for its carnivals and friendly people. It is also a good choice of wedding destination if you're nature lovers. Once part of the South American mainland, the island is blessed with Venezuelan vegetation with thick tropical rainforest, a dramatic coastline with rugged cliffs and hidden coves and remote waterfalls to bathe beneath. From March to August, you may also get a chance to see the giant leatherback turtles that swim ashore to lay their eggs, or you might like to try kayaking into the Nariva Wetlands, home of the red howler monkey, ocelots and hundreds of exotic birds.

Travel time
Around 9 hours.

Waiting period
3 working days.

Documents
- Valid 10-year passports.
- Birth certificates.

- Decree absolute (if divorced), marriage certificate and former spouse's death certificate (if widowed), adoption certificate (if adopted), deed poll proof (if name changed).
- Affidavit to prove single status.

Minimum age
18 years without parental consent.

Further information
You need to contact the office of the Registrar General, which is open from 8.30 am to 4.00 pm from Monday to Friday (see Contact details). The office must be visited at least 24 hours before the proposed wedding date in order to make an affidavit or statutory declaration and to pay a marriage fee of TT $337.50 (£33).

No ceremony can be performed after 6.00 pm in the evening. Popular locations include hotel grounds, beaches and rainforests. Ceremonies are conducted by a local minister, justice of the peace or registrar.

Weather

Lovely warm temperatures, averaging 30°C (86°F) throughout the year. The best months to visit are December though to March if you want to stay dry.

Contact details

Trinidad and Tobago Tourism Office
Mitre House, 66 Abbey Road, Bush Hill Park, Enfield, Middlesex EN1 2QE
Tel: 020 8350 1009
E-mail: Christine@ttg.co.uk

Registrar General's Office
The Red House, Abercromby Street, Port of Spain, Trinidad, West Indies
Tel: 00 1 868 623 2450

 Dream hotel
Trinidad Hilton
Lady Young Road, Port of Spain, Trinidad, West Indies
Tel: 00 1 868 624 3211
Web: www.hilton.com

This is a great place from which to explore the island and also a good choice for a wedding destination, as ceremonies are free (providing you stay the specified number of nights). It is a popular spot for couples to exchange vows, but staff will ensure that your big day feels special. The hotel sits in 175 acres of grounds and overlooks the beautiful Northern Mountain Range and picturesque Gulf of Paria, so you really feel that you've escaped to somewhere exotic. It's a large resort and pretty much everything that you could need is there, from lots of activities to a selection of restaurants serving mouth-watering international cuisine. Despite this, it's only a short taxi ride from the bustling Port of Spain where you can enjoy top-quality restaurants, bars and shops.

TURKS AND CAICOS

Couples who love their water sports will want find this group of islands irresistible. Amazingly, they aren't as well known as the nearby Bahamas, despite the fact that the diving, snorkelling and fishing are second to none and the white-sand beaches are among the world's best. Those who want to do little other than delve into the undersea world will find this a wonderful travel destination. Above sea level, the islands tend to be dry, sunny and very relaxed. The principal activity apart from water sports seems to be hanging out in the bars and restaurants along the beaches!

Travel time

Just over 11 hours to Providençiales.

Waiting period

There is a minimum residency period of 1 day in Turks and Caicos before an application for a marriage licence can be made. You must then allow 2–3 days before you can receive the licence, after which you are free to marry.

Documents

- Valid 10-year passports.
- Birth certificates.
- Decree absolute (if divorced), marriage certificate and previous spouses' death certificate (if widowed), deed poll proof (if name changed), adoption certificate (if adopted).
- A sworn affidavit must be obtained prior to your date of travel, declaring that you are both single and free to marry.
- A letter for each of you stating your occupation, marital status, age, present address and father's full name must also be produced.

DREAM HOTEL
Point Grace
PO Box 700, Providenciales, Turks and
Caicos Islands, British West Indies
Tel: 00 1 649 946 5096
E-mail: reservations@pointgrace.com

Situated on the beautiful island of
Providençiales, overlooking what
many people regard as the world's
best beach, are the secluded suites of
Point Grace. Everything about this
hotel is elegant, from the furnishings
in the bedrooms to the spacious
terraces where you can sit and watch
the sun set. It's an ideal place for a
wedding and honeymoon,
particularly their 'six-day two-year'
package, which includes a Rolls
Royce to take you to the local
church, reception, breakfast, arrival
champagne and dinner – for both
the year you marry and for your first
anniversary!

All original documents must be
presented to the registrar by the
person completing the forms.

Minimum age
21 years without parental consent. If
either of you is under 21, evidence is
required of parental consent in an
affidavit, stamped by a notary.

Further information
To obtain your marriage licence you
must apply at the Registrar General's
Office (see Contact details). The fee
for a marriage licence is US $50
(£35). If you have a specific date in
mind for your wedding, it is
advisable to make a special request
to the registrar prior to your arrival.

In Turks and Caicos, you can
choose from a traditional church
wedding ceremony, or a civil
ceremony at your hotel, the
Marriage Office or court house, or

on a beach in the sunset. For church
weddings, most ministers require
proof of membership.

Weather
There's hardly any rainfall between
November and April, and the
temperatures are consistently hot –
28–32°C (82–90°F). The wettest
period runs from June to October.

Contact details
Turks and Caicos Tourist Board
66 Abbey Road, Bush Hill Park, Enfield,
Middlesex EN1 2RQ
Tel: 020 8350 1000
Fax: 020 8350 1011
E-mail: mki@ttg.co.uk
Web: www.turksandcaicostourism.com

Marriage Officer (Grand Turks)
Registrar General's Office, Front Street,
Grand Turks, Turks and Caicos Islands,
British West Indies
Tel: 00 1 809 946 2800
Fax: 00 1 809 946 2821

Marriage Officer (Povidenciales)
c/o Chief Secretary's Office, Butterfield
Square, Providenciales, Turks and Caicos
Islands, British West Indies
Tel: 00 1 649 946 4258
Fax: 00 1 649 946 4528

Telephone numbers to arrange church weddings
Anglican: 00 1 809 946 2289
Methodist: 00 1 809 946 2115
Roman Catholic : 00 1 809 941 5136
Baptist: 00 1 809 946 2295
Faith Tabernacle: 00 1 809 946 4214
New Testament Church of God: 00 1 649
946 2175
Jehovah's Witnesses: 00 1 809 946 2532
Church of God of Prophecy: 00 1 809 946
2394
Seven Day Adventist: 00 1 809 946 2065

St Croix Trunk Bayrunk, US Virgin Islands

US VIRGIN ISLANDS

This is a favourite place for American couples to wed, but the British are less prevalent in the USVI, despite their obvious charms. There are three main islands in the group, and all the restaurants, shops and nightlife are to be found on the largest, St Thomas. St Croix is the least developed of the islands, but offers excellent diving and untouched beaches, and St John is a tiny, hilly island that offers great opportunities for hikes through the lush vegetation. There's something for every type of couple here, which makes the USVI an ideal all-year-round wedding destination.

Travel time
10 hours.

Waiting period
8 days.

Documents
• Valid 10-year passports.

• Birth certificates.
• Decree absolute (if divorced), previous spouse's death certificate (if widowed).
• Copies of documents that have been sent to the clerk of the court (see below).

Minimum age
18 years without parental consent.

Further information
You need to submit two forms in advance – an application for marriage licence and an application for licence and certificate of marriage. The applications must reach the clerk of the court (see Contact details) a minimum of two weeks prior to the wedding. Once you have completed the form, you must appear before a notary and have the application notarised before returning it to the court. The application is then posted for public inspection for an eight-day waiting

period. This can be waived if the completed application is received more than eight days before the ceremony.

Applicants should attach a letter with the applications detailing date of visit, length of stay and preferred date if they want to have the marriage performed by a judge. A date and time will be scheduled by the court on arrival of the couple wishing to marry. The court cannot make arrangements for churches. Contact should be made directly to the denomination of choice if a religious or private ceremony is to be performed. Before a marriage licence

can be issued, applicants are required to personally appear before the clerk of the court, to be questioned under oath. All fees must be paid in person – the marriage application will cost US $25 (£15), and the marriage licence US $25 (£15).

Marriages are performed from Monday to Friday except public holidays. The court will also be available on Sundays and holidays between 9.30 am and 10.30 am, by arrangement and on payment of a surcharge of US $150 (£90) per couple.

Weather

The driest period is January to May, wettest months are July to November. Temperatures are consistently hot all the year round.

Contact details

US Virgin Islands Tourist Board
Power Road Studios, 114 Power Road, Chiswick, London W4 5PY
Tel: 020 8994 0978
E-mail: usvi@destination-marketing.co.uk
Web: www.usvitourism.vi

Clerk of the Court
Territorial Court of the Virgin Islands, PO Box 70, St Thomas, US Virgin Islands 00804
Tel: 00 1 340 774 6680, ext 6607

DREAM HOTEL
Ritz-Carlton St Thomas
69000 Great Bay, St Thomas, US Virgin Islands 80802
Tel: 0800 234 000
Web: www.ritzcarlton.com

Situated within a 30-acre estate, the Ritz-Carlton St Thomas overlooks the sparkling turquoise waters and white-sand beaches of the eastern tip of the island. There's lots to do, from water sports and tennis to indulging in some delicious gourmet dining, but, equally, it's the kind of place where you can just lounge on the beach. The hotel makes an elegant wedding location. Nestled into the tranquil Great Bay, all points on the property offer panoramic views of the beautifully manicured grounds. The lush green hills of St John and the crystal-clear blue Caribbean Sea in the distance make the perfect backdrop for wedding photographs, and ceremonies can be performed on outdoor terraces or the white-sand beach.

St John, US Virgin Islands

CHAPTER 7

THE FAR EAST

The Far East is an enticing choice that offers far more than just miles of white-sand beaches lapped by crystal-clear water. In Bali, you'll discover ancient cultures, lush inland scenery and some fabulous hotels at great prices. Japan is a country of extraordinary contrasts, from the tranquility of its rural scenery to the frenetic pace of Tokyo's city life. Malaysia has a blend of Indian, Chinese and Malay traditions in everything from food to religion and architecture, making it absolutely unique. It's also a wonderful place to shop, with some amazing bargains to be had, so don't forget to pack your credit card! Thailand is also a country of many different aspects, famed for its beautiful beaches, stunning diving opportunites and awesome ancient temple sites. The people are friendly and famed for their wonderful service, and visitors come again and again, because there's so much to see. You'll probably want to go back for your first anniversary.

HEALTH TIPS

- Protection against heptatitis A, typhoid and diptheria is recommended. It may also be advisable to have injections against polio, TB, hepatitis B, rabies and Japanese B encephalitis.
- Malaria precautions are essential. Avoid mosquito bites by covering up with long sleeves and trousers, especially after sunset, and use insect repellent and a mosquito net when sleeping.

BALI

Indonesia's most beautiful island has long been a wedding and honeymoon favourite. It's the largest island in the scattering of the Indonesian archipelago, and it's easy to see why it's called the Isle of the Gods. The landscape is pure paradise, from the miles of golden-sand beaches to the lush interior of lakes, rushing rivers and rice fields carved out of the hillsides. It's popular with tourists, but there are still lots of unspoilt areas where you can discover ancient temples or deserted coves. Other reasons for Bali's popularity amongst visitors from the West include its many colourful festivals and the abundance of luxury hotels on offer. Some good spots for wedding ceremonies include the 15-acre gardens by the mile-long Legian beach in Bali.

Travel time

Around 15–16 hours via Kuala Lumpur or Singapore.

Waiting period

7 working days.

Documents

- Valid 10-year passports.
- Birth certificates.
- A certificate of no impediment, declaring that both parties are single and free to marry needs to be obtained in Denpasar (see below).
- 6 passport-size photographs of the couple to be married, sitting side by side.
- Decree absolute (if divorced), marriage certificate and previous spouse's death certificate (if widowed), deed poll proof (if name changed).

Minimum age

21 years without parental consent. If either of you is under 21, you need written proof of parental consent.

Further information

You have to visit the British Consulate in Denpasar (see Contact details) where an affidavit will be issued, which costs around £150 per couple. Couples must appear in person and swear on oath that they are free to marry.

Note: Couples used to have to travel to Jakarta for authorisation but this is no longer required, so ignore anyone who advises this.

DREAM HOTEL
The Oberoi Bali

Seminyak Beach, Jalan Laksmana, PO Box 3351 Denpasar–80033, Bali, Indonesia
Tel: 00 62 361 73 0361
E-mail: reservation@theoberoi-bali.com
Web: www.oberoihotels.com

The Oberoi Bali sits at the northern end of the vast and beautiful Legian Beach in 15 acres of exotic and manicured grounds. Couples will love the thatched roofs of the Lanai cottages and villas, which are surrounded by coral walls like a traditional Balinese village. The king-size, teak-wood beds and giant bathrooms with tubs for two are the perfect retreat for newlyweds who have just exchanged vows in this serene setting. Other features to enjoy are tennis, a gym and the large swimming pool on the edge of the beach. Vibrant Kuta with its shops and bars is just a short taxi-ride away.

🐒 DREAM HOTEL
Begawan Giri Estate
Banjar Begawan, Dusun Melinggih,
Kelod, Ubud 80571, Indonesia
Tel: 00 62 361 978888
Web: www.begawan.com

One of the world's great escapes, the Begawan Giri is a magical place for a wedding day or honeymoon. Spread over 25 acres of hillside covered in lush tropical jungle, water gardens, flowers and trees, it overlooks the Ayung River near Ubud, Bali's spiritual centre. Accommodation is in individual villas, complete with private jacuzzi and outdoor showers, and the Royal Suite has its own dining pavilion. The property is also well known for its amazing spa, The Source, where couples can indulge in massages and body wraps.

Begawan Giri Estate, Bali

If you wish to marry in a church in Bali, the bride and groom have to belong to a faith – Protestant, Roman Catholic, Muslim, Hindu or Buddhist – and both must be of the same religion. Roman Catholic couples will need to take baptism certificates, a letter of freedom to marry and a letter of delegation from your parish priest or church official.

Weather
It's consistently very hot all the year round, with temperatures averaging 31°C (88°F) and frequently rising higher from September to December. The best weather is from April to early October, with mid-October to late March being the rainy season.

Contact details
Embassy of the Republic of Indonesia
38 Grosvenor Square, London W1K 2HW
Tel: 020 7499 7661
Fax: 020 7491 4993
Web: www.indonesianembassy.org.uk

Bali Consulate Denpasar
Honorary Consul, Jl. Mertasari No. 2,
Sanur, Denpasar 80227, Bali, Indonesia
Tel: 00 62 36 270 601

 Star choice
Bali is the island where Rolling Stone Mick Jagger famously wed Jerry Hall.

JAPAN

Japan is a fascinating land of contrasts, an engaging combination of futuristic cities, ancient culture and stunning natural landscapes. From the white sandy beaches of Okinawa and the mountain hot springs of Hakone to the tranquil beauty of Kyoto and the big city excitement of Tokyo, each region of Japan has something special to offer couples. There is always something happening here and whatever your interests there is an event for you to enjoy! You can thrill to the spectacle of a Sumo tournament, experience the breathtaking colour of a fireworks festival or marvel at the ornate costumes and settings of Kabuki drama. Including an event in your travel plans offers a unique opportunity to take part in the Japanese culture.

Travel time
11 to 12 hours.

Waiting period
21 days.

Documents
- Valid 10-year passports.
- Birth certificates.
- Certificate of no impediment (see below for details).
- Decree absolute (if divorced), marriage certificate and previous spouse's death certificate (if widowed).

The document requirements can vary from area to area so it is wise to check with the ward/city office in the area where you wish to marry.

Minimum age
The male partner must be 18 years of age or older and the female partner must be 16 years of age or older. **All** persons under 20 years of age require written proof of parental consent.

Further information
Japanese law requires that all marriages must take place at a local ward or city office, where the couple must submit a notice of intention to marry *(kon-in-todoke)* beforehand. The marriage officer will then issue a certificate of acceptance of notification of marriage *(kon-in-todoke-juri-shomeisho)* and the couple can marry. Any additional ceremonies in Japan at churches, temples and so on are at the couple's discretion and are surplus to the requirements of Japanese law.

DREAM HOTEL
Windsor Hotel Toya

Shimizu Abutacho Abutagun,
Hokkaido 049–5722,
Japan
Tel: 00 81 142 731111
E-mail: info@windsor-hotels.co.jp

This grand hotel lies on a mountain between Lake Toya and the Pacific Ocean, so the views and wildlife are both spectacular. It's a truly spiritual place to tie the knot, and the little wedding chapel is perfect, with attentive staff on hand to make sure everything runs smoothly. The food here is exceptional, with mouthwatering Japanese Tsumikusa cuisine as well as French and Vietnamese fare. Come in the winter and you can go skiing in the mountains, and in the summer enjoy splashing around in the pool and going on long walks.

DREAM HOTEL
Niki Club
2301 Takakuotsu Michishita,
Nasu-machi, Nasu-gun, Tochigi-ken
325–0303, Japan
Tel: 00 81 287 782215

A wonderful little place to escape to for those in love. It's just an hour by train from Tokyo, but in a different world in terms of calm and tranquillity. It's worth a visit for the architecture alone, which is very dramatic with lots of open spaces and light. There's a wide range of things to see and do, from bathing in the natural hot springs to tennis, fishing and cycling in the surrounding countryside. The restaurant is stunning, overlooking a still pool, and the bedrooms spacious and equipped with CDs and immaculate bathrooms.

Note: To get a certificate of no impediment couples need to give notice of marriage to their local registrar in the UK. This must be displayed to the public for the prescribed period before it can be endorsed by the registrar, with 'no impediment' shown. You then need to show this UK document to a British consular officer (see Contact details) for the consular district in Japan in which you intend to marry. There are currently two consular districts – Eastern Japan and Western Japan. The consular officer will be able to issue the certificate of no impediment in Japanese as required by Japanese law. The consular fee is the equivalent of £35, payable in cash (Japanese yen) only. Although the certificate of no impediment issued by the consular officer has no expiry date, the Japanese ward or city office will normally only accept one within three months of the date of issue, as they do with the Japanese Family Register *(koseki-tohon)*. The date of issue on the certificate will be 21 days after you submit the notice of marriage.

Weather
Summer begins somewhat coolly with a rainy season but when this ends in late June, much of the country is hot and humid. Except in the far north of the country, winter in Japan is not very severe, and is usually tempered by sunshine and blue skies.

Contact details
Japan National Tourist Organisation
Heathcoat House, 20 Savile Row,
London W1S 3PR
Tel: 020 7734 9638
E-mail: info@into.co.uk
Web: www.seejapan.co.uk

British Embassy Consular Section
No 1 Lchibancho, Chiuoda-Ku, Tokyo
1028381, Japan
Tel: 00 81 3 5211 1100
E-mail: consular@tokyo.mail.fco.gov.uk
Web: www.uknow.or.jp

MALAYSIA

Malaysia is a heady mix of bustling, cosmopolitan cities such as its capital, Kuala Lumpur, mountains carpeted with jungle and rainforest and glorious beaches along the coast. It's the ultimate 'shop and flop' wedding destination, where you can flex your credit card in the well-priced arcades before heading to a fabulous deserted stretch of sand to say 'I will'.

Travel time

Around 12 hours to Kuala Lumpur, 13 hours 45 minutes to Penang.

Waiting period

7 days.

Documents

- Valid 10-year passports, accompanied by a photocopy of the data page and date of latest entry page into Malaysia.
- 1 coloured passport-size photograph.

DREAM HOTEL
Pangkor Laut Resort, Malaysia
Tel: 0800 9899 9999
E-mail: travelcentre@ytlhotels.com.my
Web: www.pangkorlautresort.com

Sitting on a privately owned island three miles off the west-coast peninsular of Malaysia, Pangkor Laut is a perfect wedding retreat. Although the island encompasses a total of 300 acres, only a fraction has been developed to house the resort and its estates while the rest is covered by lush and unspoiled rainforest, which is over two million years old. There are 148 Malaysian-style luxury villas in the main Pangkor Laut resort and eight magnificent estates in a nearby secluded cove. As the island is only accessible to the guests of the resort and estates, it makes the perfect private getaway and an ideal wedding location, and you can celebrate your special day on one of the most beautiful beaches in the world.

Malaysian Iban dance

Pan Pacific Resort, Pangkor Island, Malaysia

- Application form *Borang JPN KCO1*.
- Affidavit of marital status.
- Application form *Borang G* for marriages performed by parish or temple priests. These forms are available at the office of the registrar of marriages.
- Decree absolute (if divorced), marriage certificate and previous spouse's death certificate (if widowed).

Minimum age
21 years. If either of you is under 21, your parent(s) or legal guardian must complete consent form *Borang JPN KCO5E* which is obtainable locally or from Malaysian Embassy. You must also provide proof of guardianship, i.e. your birth certificate or guardian's custodial document.

Further information
A 'special licence' marriage speeds up the process. The application can be submitted only at the office of the registrar of marriages with form *Borang JPN KCO1*. When this form is approved by the registrar, you'll pay a small charge in cash to collect

 DREAM HOTEL
The Datai
Langkawi, Jalan Teluk Datai, Kedah Darul Aman, 07000 Pulau Langkawi, Malaysia
Web: www.langkawi-hotels.com

The Datai is situated on the north-western tip of Langkawi, providing an idyllic natural retreat within the depths of a centuries-old virgin rainforest. Set above a secluded cove, the resort has its own white-sand beach facing the peaceful Andaman Sea. Villas crafted from local materials are scattered throughout the forest and are connected to the resort's central areas by a series of pathways. It's a magical wedding location, and there are masses of romantic spots to say 'I will', from the pristine beach to the dreamy gardens.

it. The marriage will then be solemnised within seven days from the date of application. The fee for solemnising the marriage is MYR20 (£3), also to be paid in cash.

The ceremony can be performed by the registrar of marriages of the National Registration Department or by parish or temple priests who are designated as assistant registrars by the Registrar General of Marriages.

Weather
Very hot, with temperatures rarely dipping below 32°C (90°F). December to March is the best time to avoid the torrential rain that can occur at any other time.

Contact details
Registrar of Marriages, Malaysia National Registration Department, 46551 Petaling Jaya, Selangor Darul Enhsan, Malaysia
Tel: 00 60 03 7955 1255 (Marriage Department)
Fax: 00 60 03 7955 1608
Kuala Lumpur Office: 00 60 03 2692 5044

Malaysian High Commission
45 Belgrave Square, London SW1X 8QT
Tel: 020 7235 8033

 Star choice
Famous honeymooners at Malaysia's Pangkor Laut resort include James Major, the son of former prime minister John Major, and his wife, model Emma Noble, as well as film and television star Joan Collins and her latest husband, Percy Gibbons.

THAILAND
Thailand has an extraordinary range of sights to offer, from the bright lights and energy of Bangkok to the jungle in the north east and the miles of sandy beaches on its coastline. Unfortunately, if you are planning to marry in Thailand, the actual marriage ceremony has to be a purely administrative affair in Bangkok. Some travel companies and hotels will, however, arrange a further ceremony on the beach for couples wanting to say their vows in a more romantic setting.

Travel time
Around 12 hours to Bangkok.

Waiting period
4 working days.

Documents
- Valid 10-year passports.
- Birth certificates (which must show the names of both parents).
- Affidavit stating that both parties are single and free to marry.
- Decree absolute (if divorced). If the bride has been divorced less than 10 months she needs a medical certificate to confirm she is not pregnant. Marriage certificate and previous spouse's death certificate (if widowed), deed poll proof (if name changed).

Minimum age
21 years without parental consent.

Further information
Couples must register at the British Embassy in Bangkok to make an affirmation of freedom to marry. You must attend in person, bringing all of the documents listed above.

DREAM HOTEL
Amanpuri
Pansea Beach, Phuket Island, Thailand
Tel: 00 65 6887 3337
E-mail: reservations@amanresorts.com
Web: www.amanresorts.com

Amanpuri, meaning 'place of peace', was the first in the luxury Amanresort fold, and it's still one of the best for honeymooners. Built around a coconut grove above a white-sand beach, it boasts a first-class spa, its own cruise boat fleet and a plethora of water sports. Each of the 40 Thai-style pavilions and private villa homes are blissful. Newlyweds will love the king-size beds and sunbeds for lazing on. It's a very laid-back resort: dining is as formal or as casual as you like, but the torch-lit beach barbecues are a must.

The affirmation can be administered between 1.00 pm and 3.30 pm from Monday to Thursday and costs 2,100 baht (£332). When the affirmation has been granted, it must be translated into Thai. The staff at the embassy will be able to advise on where you can get this done. You will also require authentication of the British consular official's signature and certification of the Thai translation, which you can get from the Department of Consular Affairs (see Contact details). It can take up to two full days for the ministry to process the application. When this is done, the affirmation should be submitted to the district registrar who will issue a Thai marriage certificate.

As this procedure doesn't involve a ceremony, you may want to arrange a more romantic exchange of vows afterwards, such as a traditional morning blessing by Buddhist monks (all ceremonies conducted by a monk must take place before 11.00 am on any given day).
Note: A religious ceremony on its own is not sufficient – you will not be legally married.

Weather
Tropical and humid, with average temperatures around 32°C (90°F). Thailand is most comfortable from November to February after which temperatures really start to climb.

 DREAM HOTEL
Tongsai Bay Cottages and Hotel
84 Moo 5, Bophut Beach, Koh Samui, Thailand
Tel: 00 66 77 425 015

The Tongsai Bay Cottages and Hotel is the only resort in Koh Samui that can claim to have its own secluded beach, and at 200 miles long it never gets crowded. This is a beach-worshippers' paradise – no beach vendors, dogs or passers-by, just you and your partner. Honeymooners should head for the aptly named Lovers' Corner situated at the right-hand end, which is a great location for a marriage blessing! The Tongsai Bay Cottages are set in 25 acres of beautiful gardens full of flowers and are exquisite inside, but the 'wow' factor is the balcony, which features an open-air bathtub where you can sit and soak while you gaze at the pretty bay below.

The rainy season is from June to November and the driest time to go is March to December.

Contact details

Consular Section
British Embassy, 1031 Wireless Road, Bangkok 10330
Tel: 00 66 0 2305 8333, ext 2217
E-mail:
Vacharee.Tumronggrachaniti@fco.gov.uk
Web: www.britishemb.or.th

The Legalisation Division/ Department of Consular Affairs
123 Chaeng Wattana Road, Laksi District, Bangkok 11120, Thailand
Tel: 00 66 0 575 105659

Opposite: Sydney Harbour, Australia

A klong in Bangkok, Thailand

CHAPTER 8
THE ANTIPODES AND THE PACIFIC

A ustralia has, quite simply, got the lot: from lush coastal plains to dramatic red rocks inland, from spectacular coral reefs to snow-covered mountains, from remote bush and sophisticated cities. If you're an active couple, you'll want to indulge in diving, bush walking, surfing or hiking in the mountains. If you're the shop-and-flop type, Sydney with its plethora of hotels, shops, theatres, bars and fabulous harbour and beaches is a must-visit.

New Zealand is a haven of unspoilt tranquillity where you'll discover amazing locations to exchange your vows, from dense forests or towering mountains to vast glaciers.

The Pacific islands are lapped by warm waters and blessed with near-constant sunshine. What's more, the exotic blend of Polynesian, Malay, French, Indian and Chinese cultures guarantees that you're going to experience fabulous cuisine.

HEALTH TIPS

- No injections are needed for visiting Australia or New Zealand. However, you'll need a yellow fever certificate if you're entering within six days of leaving an infected area.

- For the Pacific Islands, you may be advised to have yourself innoculated against hepatitis A and typhoid.

- The main protection you'll need is against the sun. Be sure to pack a high SPF sun cream and take a hat. You may also need insect repellent, although malaria is not present.

AUSTRALIA

With its abundance of romantic wedding destinations, Australia makes an exciting place to tie the knot. It's a vast, exciting country and a land of amazing variety. You can go from the alpine grandeur of the Snowy Mountains to the breathtaking isolation of the outback and marvel at natural wonders such as Ayers Rock (now known by its Aboriginal name, Ururu). Head up to Queensland and you'll find you're in a sub-tropical climate with rainforests, bush trails and waterfalls to discover, not forgetting the world-famous Great Barrier Reef. If it's city culture that you're after, there's Sydney with its famous landmarks such as the Harbour Bridge and the opera house. Lively couples will find lots to see and do in this lively metropolis, from hanging out in the great restaurants and bars, to taking a cruise around the bay.

Travel time
About 20 hours to Sydney.

Waiting period
1 working day.

Documents
- Valid 10-year passports.
- Birth certificates.
- Decree absolute (if divorced), marriage certificate and previous spouse's death certificate (if widowed), deed poll proof (if name changed).
- A certificate of intention to marry is also required, available from the Australian High Commission in London (see Contact details).

DREAM HOTEL
Lilianfels Blue Mountains
Lilianfels Avenue, Echo Point, Katoomba, New South Wales 2780, Australia
Tel: 00 61 02 4780 1200
E-mail: reservations@lilianfels.com.au

Only a 90-minute drive from Sydney, Lilianfels Blue Mountains is one of Australia's finest boutique hotels. Its location in the heart of the World-Heritage-listed Blue Mountains National Park is superb, offering views of the towering peaks and deep blue-hazed valleys of The Three Sisters. It's very tranquil, set in two acres of cottage-style gardens and the 85 rooms, which have recently been refurbished, are a great mix of modern comfort and country house chic, with wood floors, soft rugs and large windows for light and space; some have four-poster beds too. There's also a spa and several function rooms, ideal for post-wedding celebrations.

- An affidavit stating that both parties are single and free to marry.

Minimum age
18 years without parental consent.

Further information
Weddings are conducted from Monday to Friday, excluding public holidays. There is an extraordinary range of places to marry here, including some unusual ones, such as the steps of the Sydney Opera House (see Chapter 12).

Weather
Broadly there are two climatic zones. About 40 per cent of

Australia lies in the tropical zone – this is in the north of the country, above the Tropic of Capricorn, where temperatures average 26°C (80°F) June to August and top 30°C (87°F) November to March. The remaining areas lie in the temperate zone, where generally speaking, the seasons are the opposite of those of the northern hemisphere, with average temperatures ranging from 17°C (63°F) in the winter to well over 26°C (80°F) in the summer.

Contact details

Australian Tourist Commission
Gemini House, 10–18 Putney Hill, London
SW15 6AA
Tel: 020 8780 2229
Web: www.australia.com

Australian High Commission
Strand, London WC2B 4LA
Tel: 020 7379 4334
Web: www.australia.org.uk

Wedding organisers

Weddings By Design
Shop 11, 99–111 Military Road,
Neutral Bay, Sydney Suburbs 2000,
New South Wales, Australia
Tel: 00 61 29 90 44765

DREAM HOTEL
Haggerstone Island
PO Box 153H, Edge Hill,
Queensland 4870, Australia
Tel: 00 61 740 603413
Web: www.haggerstoneisland.com

This is an extraordinary retreat, set on its own uninhabited island, surrounded by the hundreds of untouched reefs, sand cays and jungle islands of the northern Great Barrier Reef, about 400 miles north of Cairns. It's a number one spot for newlyweds as it's incredibly private – a real once-in-a-lifetime destination. The food is freshly picked or caught on the island every day, the accommodation is built of hand-hewn wood, and the panoramic views out to sea are stupendous. The huge beds have crisp cotton sheets and the bathrooms have slate floors, with one glass wall offering incredible views. One rustic hut even has an outside shower and toilet for a real back-to-nature vibe. Honeymooners should indulge in a candlelit dinner on one of the sandy cays. Robinson Crusoe – eat your heart out.

Uluru (Ayers Rock), Australia

COOK ISLANDS

The Cook Islands are a beach-lovers' paradise. They consist of 15 islands scattered over some 1.5 million square miles of the warm Pacific Ocean lying virtually in the centre of the Polynesian Triangle of the South Pacific, flanked to the west by the kingdom of Tonga and the Samoas, and to the east by Tahiti and the island of French Polynesia. Rarotonga is the largest of the islands and hosts the international airport, and Avarua, the main township, has a good choice of restaurants, shops, hotels and banks. There are lots of wedding locations to choose, from lush tropical gardens scented with exotic flowers to sandy white beaches lapped by turquoise waters.

Travel time

20–22 hours via Los Angeles.

 DREAM HOTEL
Manuia Beach Boutique Hotel
PO Box 700 Rorotonga, Cook Islands
Tel: 00 68 2 22461
E-mail: room@manuia.co.ck
Web: www.manuia.co.uk

Situated on a beautiful white sandy beach overlooking a sparkling lagoon, this secluded hotel is a lovely place for a marriage ceremony amid tropical landscaped gardens. You will spend your first night of married life together in one of 20 individually decorated, Polynesian-style thatched *are* (bungalows), each with a veranda where you can sit and gaze out to sea.

Cook Islands

Waiting period

3 working days.

Documents

- Valid 10-year passports.
- Birth certificates.
- Decree absolute (if divorced).

Minimum age

20 years. If either of you is under 20, written proof of consent of both parents is required.

Further information

An application for a marriage licence must be made in person to the registrar of marriages in the Cook Islands on arrival (see Contact details). An application for this licence cannot be made outside the Cook Islands. The marriage licence costs US $50 (£30), a marriage certificate US $15 (£9).

You can marry in any one of the many stunningly beautiful outside locations, or you may prefer just a simple ceremony beside your hotel swimming pool. There are also lots of churches on the islands of various demoninations including Protestant, Church of Jesus Christ and Latter Day Saints, Seventh Day Adventist and Roman Catholic. It is necessary to check with the minister of the church you choose, regarding the local requirements to marry in a church, and you are likely to need written consent from them.

Weather

The climate in the Cook Islands is tropical. Summer, between December and April, is hotter and more humid with a higher risk of tropical storms and sometimes cyclones. Winter is between May and November.

Contact details

Cook Islands Tourist Board
Hillsbalfour, 36 Southwark Bridge Road, London SE1 9EU
Tel: 020 7922 1100

Registrar's Department
Department of Justice and Lands,
PO Box 11 Rarotonga, Cook Islands
Tel: 00 68 229410
Fax: 00 68 229610
E-mail: offices@justice.gov.ck

DREAM HOTEL
Pacific Resort Rarotonga
PO Box 790 Rarotonga, Cook Islands
Web: www.pacificresort.com

Exclusively located on the edge of Rarotonga's finest lagoon, this luxury hotel arranges weddings on an individual basis. The accommodation is made for honeymooners, including 46 one- and two-bedroomed apartments and seven luxurious villas located either in the garden or by the lagoon. This is the place to come if you want to laze around on a fantastic white-sand beach and be waited on hand and foot. There are things to do if you feel inclined, such as kayaking, canoeing, rowing and snorkelling, or you can take a lagoon cruise with snorkelling followed by an island barbecue lunch.

FIJI

If the South Pacific conjures up for you images of islands with swaying palms and deserted golden beaches lapped by warm sea, you'd be right. And if your idea of a perfect wedding destination comes straight from the Bounty Bar adverts, then this is the place for you. Fiji consists of dozens of tiny reef-ringed islands dotted across the warm waters of the South Pacific and is well known for its deserted beaches and great diving. It's also remarkably free of tourists – so far.

Travel time

Around 21 hours 30 minutes.

Waiting period

1 working day.

Documents

- Valid 10-year passports.
- Original birth certificates.
- Decree absolute (if divorced), previous spouse's death certificate (if widowed), adoption certificate (if adopted), deed poll proof (if name changed).

Minimum age

21 years without parental consent. If either of you is under 21, you need officially witnessed written proof of the consent of your father.

Further information

Couples need to go to the register office together when applying for the licence. There are offices in Suva, Nadi and Lautoka. When marrying at Namale Resort, Cousteau or Lomalagi, registration must be completed at Savusavu. For Matagi, Qamea, Maravu, and Taveuni, you will register on

Taveuni. Registration offices are open between 9.00 am and 3.00 pm, from Monday to Friday, and the registration formalities take about 15 minutes. The fee is FJ $20 (£6) and the licence is valid for 21 days.

There are no non-denominational ministers in Fiji. For Roman Catholic weddings, the requirements include a letter of freedom to marry, sent 2–3 months in advance to the Fijian priest, along with your baptism certificates. You should complete your normal pre-wedding studies in the UK and take a letter from your priest to confirm this.

Weather

Fiji enjoys an ideal tropical climate with delightful average temperatures of 29°C (85°F). It can get pretty hot in the summer but temperatures seldom go above 32°C (90°F). Trade winds from the east and south-east bring cooling breezes in the late afternoon and early evening, all the year round.

Contact details

Fiji Tourist Board
36 Southwark Bridge Road, London SE1 9EU
Tel: 020 7922 1100
E-mail: info@hillsbalfour.com
Web: www.bulafiji.com

Fiji Visitors' Bureau
Thomson Street, PO Box 92 Suva, Fiji
Tel: 00 67 9 330 2433
E-mail: infodesk@fijifvb.gov.fj
Web: www.BulaFiji.com

Registrar of Births, Deaths and Marriages
PO Box 2236, Government Buildings, Suva, Fiji

 DREAM HOTEL
Turtle Island Resort
Turtle Island Sales Office, Suite A-1, 10906 NE 39th Street, Vancouver WA 98682–6789, USA
Tel: 00 1 360 256 4347
Web: www.designhotels.com

Routinely voted one of the world's best destinations, Turtle Island is faultless for wedding and honeymoon couples – providing you adore sun, soft sand and sunsets. This retreat, which is a member of the Design Hotels group, is all your desert island fantasies rolled into one. It's also where the sultry *Blue Lagoon* movie was made! There's only accommodation for 14 couples on the 500-acre, privately owned island, so it's an ideal hideaway. Weddings are fabulous: you can say 'I will' at a traditional Fijian ceremony held at sunset on the shores of the famous Blue Lagoon.

 DREAM HOTEL
Vatulele Island Resort
Fiji
Tel: 00 61 2 9665 8700 (Worldwide reservations, Sydney)
E-mail: info@vatulele.com
Web: www.vatulele.com

Set on a private 60-acre island, this exclusive resort is a superb wedding destination. The marriage ceremony is usually held on the beach at sunset, in a church with doors and windows created from plaited coconut leaves and flowers. Traditionally dressed Fijian warriors accompany the bride on a barge trip across the lagoon, and children toss flower petals in the sand as she is carried ashore to take her vows.

NEW ZEALAND

New Zealand has such a diverse range of attractions, your biggest problem will be deciding which of the two main islands (North Island or South Island) to head for. From glaciers and carpets of tropical rainforests to ancient volcanoes and acres of rolling grasslands as far as the eye can see, New Zealand is a nature at its finest. It's also where bungee-jumping first started, so if you're a fan of extreme sports, you'll find ample opportunities to indulge yourself here. Then there are the unspoilt beaches that line the coasts and the bustling cities such as Wellington and Auckland to explore. Getting married here is a pretty easy process too: once you've completed and lodged a notice of intended marriage and got the go-ahead, you can get planning!

Travel time
Around 23 hours.

Waiting period
3 days.

Documents
- Valid 10-year passports.
- Birth certificates.
- Affidavit stating that both parties are single and free to marry.
- Decree absolute (if divorced), marriage certificate and previous spouse's death certificate (if widowed).

Urupukapuka Island, New Zealand

DREAM HOTEL
Wharekauhau Country Estate
Western Lake Road, Palliser Bay, RD3
Featherston, Wairarapa, New Zealand
Tel: 00 64 6 307 7581
Fax: 00 64 6 307 7799
E-mail:
reservations@wharekauhau.co.nz
Web: www.wharekauhau.co.nz

Frequently listed among the top 20 international resort hideaways, Wharekauhau on North Island is the perfect wedding location or honeymoon destination. It is located on a 5,000-acre working sheep station overlooking the spectacular Palliser Bay with views of cloud-capped mountains and forests. Visitors here can choose from a wide range of outdoor activities such as quad bikes, clay target shooting, horse riding and jet-boating, or simply indulge in its splendid luxury, superb local wines and irresistible cuisine. Each day ends in a sumptuous cottage with panoramic views of the nearby ocean.

Minimum age
20 years. If either of you is under 20, written proof of parental consent is required.

Further information
In New Zealand you must be married by a registered marriage celebrant. This may be a registrar of marriages, a civil marriage celebrant, a minister of a church or a person connected with an approved organisation. You will need to contact your chosen celebrant to agree on a time and place before applying for your marriage licence.

Canterbury Plains, New Zealand

To get a licence, you must complete application form BDM58 (notice of intended marriage for parties ordinarily resident outside New Zealand). You can download the form from the website www.bdm.govt.nz (see also Contact details).

As part of completing the application form, one of you must make a formal statutory declaration that there is no lawful impediment to the marriage, i.e. no legal reason that you cannot marry. Once you have completed this, signed the statutory declaration and had it witnessed, you send the form to the New Zealand registrar of marriages closest to where you intend to marry. You should also advise the registrar of the date that you intend to collect the marriage licence. This must be at least three days after your completed form reaches the registry, so do allow plenty of time.

You are free to marry at the place specified on the marriage licence. If you wish to be married by a Registrar of Births, Deaths and Marriages at the register office, you must pay a fee of NZ $120 (£40), which includes the fee for the marriage licence. For ceremonies conducted by a minister or civil celebrant in places other than a registry office the licence fee is NZ $80 (£28). The celebrant must be registered to conduct marriages in New Zealand and their name must be given on the form in order for your licence to be issued. The marriage licence is valid for three months from the date on which it is issued.

Weather

South Island has a temperate climate similar to the UK but with the seasons the opposite way round. The best months to visit for sun are from December to February. North Island has a subtropical climate with average temperatures rising to over 26°C (80°F).

Contact details

Central Registry
Births Deaths and Marriages,
PO Box 10–526 Wellington,
47 Boulcott Street, Wellington,
New Zealand
Tel: 00 64 04 474 8150
E-mail: bdm.nz@dia.govt.nz
Web: www.bdm.govt.nz

DREAM HOTEL
Grasmere Lodge
State Highway 73, Cass, Canterbury,
Private Bag 55009 Christchurch,
New Zealand
Tel: 00 64 3 318 8407
Fax: 00 64 3 318 8263
E-mail: retreat@grasmere.co.nz
Web: www.grasmere.co.nz

Historic Grasmere Lodge, nestled in the mountains of New Zealand's South Island, is a country boutique retreat so full of charm you'll never want to leave. This traditional New Zealand ranch, set in 13,000 acres amid towering 7,000-foot peaks, is a haven for romantics who want to hide away, but also a wonderland for couples seeking adventure. Open fireplaces dominate the large panelled lounge and den, which has many books on the history of the region. The fine cuisine of Grasmere Lodge uses the best local ingredients including venison, beef, lamb and salmon. Trout caught by guests often feature on the menu, along with seasonal delicacies such as West Coast whitebait and Kaikoura crayfish (lobster). The lodge has an extensive cellar of award-winning New Zealand wines. All of Grasmere's ten guest bedrooms are individually decorated, and have lots of luxurious extras and jacuzzi baths. A perfect wedding destination, particularly if you take over the whole lodge with family and friends!

THE USA AND MEXICO

A land as diverse as North America has no end of places for you to exchange your wedding vows. How about the bay of San Francisco, or the top of the Empire State Building? Or barefoot romance on the golden beaches of California or the breathtaking Grand Canyon? Of course, the USA is home to the city of sin, Las Vegas, where celebrities have flocked for years to tie the knot in super-kitsch style. If you fancy following the footsteps of Elvis, then this is for you!

Mexico is a fun and exotic place to wed: the shimmering beaches, the buzzy nightlife and glitzy hotels of Cancun are particularly popular and the bustle of Mexico City is not to be missed. But if you fancy somewhere a little more romantic and secluded, head for the unspoilt east coast, where spectacular scenery and untouched beaches will enchant you.

HEALTH TIPS

- One of the beauties of travelling to the USA is that there is little threat of disease, so no vaccinations are necessary. Comprehensive medical insurance is essential, however.

- In Mexico there is more risk, so you are recommended to have boosters of tetanus and courses of hepatitis A and typhoid. It may also be advisable to have courses for diptheria, tuberculosis, rabies and hepatitis B.

ALASKA

For the ultimate alternative wedding destination, look no further than Alaska, the USA's most northerly state. If exchanging vows in the sunshine on a golden beach is not for you, but getting married in a rustic lodge overlooking some of the most wild, unspoilt countryside in the world sounds appealing, then Alaska could be the ideal wedding destination for you. Your trip of a lifetime could include a visit to the beautiful Kenai Fjords and horse riding in the Kenai National Wildlife Refuge. Or you could take a flight over an ice field or a trip to a watching site to view the famous Alaskan brown bears fishing in one of the area's fast-flowing rivers. Or you may want to have a go at canoeing or kayaking. There's no end to the exhilarating activities that you can do in this glorious state, including getting hitched!

Travel time

10 hours.

Waiting period

3 working days, unless you've applied for a marriage licence by post in advance, in which case you can marry straight away.

Documents

- Valid 10-year passports.
- Decree absolute (if divorced and your previous marriage ended within 60 days of your application), marriage certificate and previous spouse's death certificate (if widowed).

Opposite: Indian Canyon, California

 DREAM HOTEL

Pearson's Pond Luxury Inn and Adventure Spa

4541 Sawa Circle, Juneau, Alaska 99801, USA
Tel: 00 1 907 789 3772
E-mail: book@pearsonspond.com

Nestled in Alaska's 1,000-mile coastal passage where the mountains meet the sea is Pearson's Pond, the ultimate rural retreat. It's a fabulously romantic spot, where one of the most popular weddings sites is the Lakeside Marriage Arch on a floating, flower-filled dock. A fountain, wild ducks, beautiful gardens and views of the world-famous Mendenhall Glacier and mountains provide a picturesque backdrop that will live in your memories forever. The Atrium Lounge in the lodge is another popular location, perfect for an indoor ceremony and small reception, complete with fireplace, cathedral ceilings with chandeliers and floor-to-ceiling windows overlooking the forest. The lounge is a good choice if you're worried about the Alaskan weather. Unparalleled scenery and spectacular natural beauty are close by, most notably the Mendenhall Glacier, Eaglecrest Ski Area and Pack Creek at Admiralty Island National Park, and if you feel like relaxing, there's access to the great adventure spa where you can be pampered in style.

Minimum age

18 years without parental consent. If either of you is under 18, you should contact the Bureau of Vital Statistics (see Contact details) for additional instructions.

Further information

There is a three-day waiting period before a licence can be granted. An application can be made in person, by phone, fax or letter. The waiting period begins once the necessary information is received. If your application is made by phone or fax a hard copy of the information must follow by mail.

You must provide full names, addresses and telephone numbers for both of you plus all the appropriate documents listed above. Once your licence has been issued it is valid for 90 days. You can also obtain the application form online (go to www.dced.state.ak.us) and fax it to the relevant marriage bureau.

 DREAM HOTEL
Afognak Wilderness Lodge
Seal Bay, Alaska 99697, USA
Tel: 00 1 907 486 6442
E-mail: afognak@usa.net
Web: www.afognaklodge.com

As wild and remote as you could wish for, Afognak is as an adventurous place to marry. It's located on the mountainous and densely forested Afognak Island, which is part of the Kodiak group, situated just off Alaska's south coast and well known for their amazing wildlife. Stay here, and you'll get a chance to go whale-watching and see brown bears feeding on salmon, sea lions basking on the rocks and herds of elk moving through the forests. With three guest cabins, each with two bedrooms and spacious living rooms, it's an ideal place to take over for a whole wedding if you want some family and friends to come.

You will be required to appear in person at one of the marriage bureaus with your passports.

Your wedding ceremony may be held anywhere on land so you can choose anything from a glacier field (travel there by helicopter!) to a chapel on a lake or one of the many spectacular glacier gardens. If you want a religious service, contact the church of your choice direct. Details of churches are obtainable from Alaska Tourism (see below).

Weather

A very varied climate, with interesting extremes. The sea currents of the warm Pacific keep the coastal areas fairly mild throughout the year with temperatures rarely dropping below 10°C (50°F), although rainfall is high and there can be a lot of fog. In the mountains and inland the winters are snowy and bitterly cold, summers June to August are hot.

Contact details

American Embassy
24 Grosvenor Square, London W1A 1AE
Tel: 020 7499 9000

Alaska Tourism
1st Floor, Stamford House, Woodbridge Road, Guildford, Surrey
Tel: 01483 457177
Fax: 01483 451361

Alaska Division of Tourism
Web: www.dced.state.ak.as

For a list of marriage bureaux

Bureau of Vital Statistics
PO Box 110675, Juneau,
Alaska 99811–0675, USA
Tel: 00 1 907 465 3038
Fax: 00 1 907 465 3618

ARIZONA

Fancy getting married in one of America's – if not the world's – most famous natural attractions? That's right, Arizona is home to the Grand Canyon, which never fails to impress even the most well-travelled adventurer. You could marry at the popular South Rim, which offers panoramic views and gives a true impression of its sheer size, or you could just jump into a helicopter and exchange your vows mid-air, looking down on the canyon! Of course, the Grand Canyon isn't all Arizona has to offer. Other delights include the varied landscapes, which take in tall mountain ranges, raging rivers, grasslands, desert sand dunes and cactus forests. Above all, it's a land of extremes. In just a few hours, you can leave the desert behind and head up into the San Francisco Peaks to the snowbowl, where you can indulge in a spot of skiing or snowboarding.

Of course, there's another side to Arizona, which is the glitzy, glamorous city of Las Vegas, which is famous for its casinos and also as a favourite wedding location. The choice of wedding styles and venues there is so extraordinary that I've given it a section of its own, starting on page 151.

Travel time
Around 9 hours.

Waiting period
None specified.

Documents
● Photo ID (either driver's licence with photograph or passport).

 DREAM HOTEL
The Boulders
PO Box 2090, 34631 North Tom Darlington Drive, Carefree, Arizona 85377, USA
Tel: 00 1 602 488 9009

The Boulders is remarkable place to have a wedding ceremony. Set out in the Soran Desert, to the north east of Phoenix, its 160 rooms, or *casitas,* are made of red stone that has been moulded and rubbed down to match the existing large boulders of the area. The effect is astonishing, as the resort perfectly blends in with its surroundings. Each of the *casitas* features a wood-burning fireplace, large tiled bathroom, stone floors and private patio overlooking the desert. Weddings here are on an individual basis, so you can be as low-key as you like. Its other attractions include a private country club with two 18-hole championship courses built right into the desert, tennis garden and the Sonoran Spa (with the Golden Door Spa coming soon). For the fitness-minded, the resort boasts several desert trail hikes, mountain-biking and nature walks. Five restaurants all serving up different international cuisine are the icing on the cake.

Minimum age
18 years without parental consent. If either of you is under 18, you need written proof of parental consent. 16- to 17-year-olds need a notarised parental consent form signed by your parents. Your parents may accompany you and present proper identification and may sign the parental consent form in front of the clerk issuing the licence. Anyone under 16 will need a court order as

well as a notarised parental consent form as mentioned above.

Further information

You may obtain a marriage licence in any county in Arizona (contact details below) as long as your wedding is to take place in Arizona. There is no waiting period and you may marry as soon as you have received the licence. The licence expires one year from the date of issue. Both of you must be present to apply and the licence costs US $50 (£30).

There are lots of fun wedding options in Arizona. Very popular is a helicopter wedding, where the bride and groom enjoy a helicopter ride and then land for a private ceremony in a secluded spot such as Red Rocks in the Grand Canyon.

Wranglers in Arizona

DREAM HOTEL
Arizona Biltmore Resort and Spa

24th Street and Missouri Avenue, Phoenix, Arizona 8016, USA
Tel: 0800 950 0086

Known throughout the world as the 'Jewel of the Desert,' the Arizona Biltmore Resort and Spa in the heart of Phoenix provides a restful oasis of 39 acres covered with lush gardens, glistening swimming pools and Frank Lloyd Wright-influenced architecture. Weddings are held throughout the pretty grounds, with the Aztec Patio a favourite spot as it overlooks a fountain and can accommodate up to 150 guests. The 500 bedrooms and suites all have private patios or balconies, overlooking the gardens with their pool and fountains, and with views of Squaw Peak Mountain in the distance.

If you do want to opt for a more unusual location, you'll need to pay usage fees, which vary for each location, and a free marriage permit from the National Park Service is required.

Weather

The desert areas (in the southern half of the state) are extremely hot. The cooler time lasts from January through to March, whilst in the mountainous regions (in the

Star choice
The Arizona Biltmore has been a favourite of celebrities and US presidents throughout its colourful history – former US president Ronald Reagan and his wife Nancy honeymooned there.

northern half of the state) the best time to visit is from June through to August.

Contact details

Arizona Office of Tourism
PO Box 25458, Phoenix, Arizona 85002, USA
Tel: 00 1 602 230 7733
Brochure request line: 0906 5770031
Web: www.arizonaguide.com

Arizona wedding websites

www.ArizonaWeddings.com
www.SedonaWeddings.com
www.uniqueweddings.net
www.weddingsinsedona.com
www.allweddingcompanies.com

Palm Springs Hotel, California

CALIFORNIA

With its beaches, sunny climate, great restaurants and fabulous cities to explore, California really is a great place to head for your wedding day. Pretty much anything goes in this state, so whether you've dreamed of saying 'I will' with sand beneath your toes, by a picturesque lake or in the middle of the desert, it's all possible here. There's plenty to see and do in this lively state, and whether you are the outdoor type or a shopaholic, you'll find more than enough to keep you entertained. Choose from remote wilderness, monster roller-coasters, famous landmarks, intriguing exhibitions or endangered animals. Of course if you both love the movies, then you'll want to head to Los Angeles. You could even end up tying the knot at a location used for your favourite film! California is also famous for its wine: around 90 per cent of the USA's wine is produced in the state, so there should be ample opportunities to toast your new life together.

Travel time

Around 10 hours 30 minutes to Los Angeles, San Francisco or San Diego.

Waiting period

Non specified.

Documents

- Valid 10-year passports.
- Birth certificates.
- Decree absolute (if divorced).

Minimum age

18 years without parental consent. If either of you is under 18, you must have written proof of consent of a parent or legal guardian.

DREAM HOTEL
Four Seasons Biltmore, Santa Barbara

1260 Channel Drive, Santa Barbara,
California 93108, USA
Tel: 0800 332 3442

A gem of a hotel, built in the 1920s, that has long attracted the rich and famous looking for a romantic getaway, like film stars Michael Douglas and Michelle Pfeiffer. Situated in 22 acres overlooking the Pacific Ocean, there are 234 rooms and 12 luxury suites in charming cottages with white shutters and pretty flower-filled gardens. A real treat is a romantic meal in The Patio, a gorgeous restaurant, which has a glass roof with retractable panels that are opened up if the weather's good. There's also an Olympic-sized pool to laze by and horse riding and sailing if you're feeling more energetic.

Further information

You will have to obtain a marriage licence. This is simple – just go to any county courthouse in the state and show valid identification, pay around US $40–60 (£24–36) and then get married straight away. No blood test is required.

In California it's possible to have any type of wedding ceremony so you're not restricted to a civil service. You can get married in church, at the courthouse, on the beach, in the mountains, even underwater while scuba-diving. The most popular venues for weddings include a chapel in the Yosemite National Park, South Lake Tahoe's 35 wedding chapels and lakeside resorts, such as Zephyr Cove Resort

 Star choice
If you stay in one of California's smart hotels, you will almost certainly spot some famous faces. For example, Meg Ryan and Dennis Quaid walked up the aisle at the Hotel Bel Air.

and the Del Coronado Hotel in San Diego. There are also venues on the Monterey Peninsula, such as The Highlands Inn, The Lodge at Pebble Beach, Stonepine Resort, San Francisco, The Disneyland Hotel in Anaheim and Napa Valley.

Weather

Spring and autumn are the best seasons to visit California as those have the best mixture of benign climate, hotel availability and scenic splendour.

 DREAM HOTEL
Hotel Bel Air

701 Stone Canyon Road, Los Angeles,
California 90077, USA
Tel: 0800 648 4097

A Mediterranean-style hideaway in the exclusive Bel Air district, this hotel has a real air of old Hollywood about it. It's an extremely popular choice for summer weddings. Lots of couples choose to marry overlooking the picturesque Swan Lake, which is surrounded by flowers and has a pretty bridge spanning it. After the ceremony, newlyweds can enjoy complete privacy in the 11 acres of landscaped gardens and courtyards with fountains, a giant oval swimming pool and guest villas. Nice touches include open fireplaces and private patios.

🏹 DREAM HOTEL
The Willows
412 West Tahquitz Canyon Way, Palm
Springs, California 92262, USA
Tel: 00 1 760 320 0771
Web: www.thewillowspalmsprings.com

This Mediterranean-style, eight-bedroomed, antique-filled villa is just as popular with stars today as it was when in first opened in the 1950s. The likes of Cameron Diaz have been known to be seen here, relaxing by the sparkling 1930s-style pool and enjoying the fragrant frangipani-filled gardens. Ceremonies can take place in either The Courtyard, which has natural air-conditioning in the form of a waterfall, or The Living Room, both of which can seat up to 100 guests for ceremony and reception. Bedrooms are individually decorated to a standard that makes this one of the most seductive hotels in the West. The pick of the bunch is the Marion Davies Room, which has an elegantly carved king-sized bed and a chaise longue and silver chandelier in the bathroom!

Contact details

California Tourism Office
Tel: 0906 577 0032
Web: www.visitcalifornia.com

The Palm Springs Bureau of Tourism
Web: www.palm-springs.org (also has a link
to ww.info@weddingconcierge.info)

Los Angeles Convention and
Visitors' Bureau
Main Office, 2400 Imperial Highway,
Norwalk, Los Angeles
Tel: 00 1 562 462 2137
Web: www.lacvb.com

Useful websites

Web: Richard@psYoureInvited.com
Web: www.weddingspalmsprings.com

COLORADO

Steeped in tradition, Colorado is true cowboy country and the place to head if you're looking for an adventure wedding in America's Wild West. Most of the state of Colorado is above 6,000 feet, so its mountainous landscape, including the Rocky Mountain National Park, dominates the land and makes for a truly dramatic and exhilarating destination. It also provides some of the world's best skiing and snowboarding experiences in the world, so it's a great place to head if you want a real 'white' wedding! Colorado is the home of exclusive resort Aspen, as well as Winter Park Resort, Silver Creek and Berthoud Pass. Other fun snow pursuits to enjoy while you're there include snowshoeing, snowmobiling and cross-country skiing on backcountry trails. For a unique experience, you can also take a dip in the hot spring pools at Grand Lake and Hot Sulphur Springs.

Travel time
Around 10 hours.

Waiting period
None specified.

Documents
- Valid 10-year passports.
- Birth certificates.
- Decree absolute (if divorced), marriage certificate and previous spouse's death certificate (if widowed).

Minimum age
18 years without parental consent. If you are 16 or 17, you will need written proof of the consent of both your parents (or single parent having

🕊 DREAM HOTEL
Canyon Crest Lodge
Yeoman Drive, Pagosa Springs,
Colorado 81147, USA
Tel: 00 1 970 731 3773
Web: www.canyoncrestlodge.com
E-mail: canyoncrest@pagosa.net

This beautiful stone-and-log house in the San Juan Mountains is set in an incredibly romantic location, surrounded by 38 acres of tall pines. It's a real hideaway, and the staff take great delight in arranging weddings of all kinds, from intimate little ceremonies to lavish parties where couples take over the whole lodge. It makes a wonderful wedding-night venue too.

legal custody) or guardian, or seek judicial approval. It is possible to marry if you are under 16, but a judicial court order is necessary as well as written parental consent.

Aspen, Colorado

Further information
Both the bride and groom must appear in person to apply for the marriage licence, and must bring all necessary documents (see above). You will need to have a witness with you when you sign the marriage licence application, so you may want to bring your maid of honour or best man with you. The bride will need to say what her married name will be when she signs the application, and that name must also match the name she signs on the marriage licence.

The marriage licence must be given to the officiant on your wedding day. After the ceremony, he or she will sign it and send it to the proper government agency for validation. The marriage licence is valid for 30 days and can only be used within the State of Colorado. Pretty much anything goes here in terms of the style of ceremony – you can include civil or religious readings, and interfaith ceremonies are allowed. The choice of location is also very wide, from hotels to churches and even mountain-tops.

Weather
Noted for its excellent climate, the air here is normally exceptionally crisp and clear. Summers are pleasantly warm and very sunny and dry. In the winter the mountains are naturally snowy but extreme cold rarely lasts more than a few days even in the depths of winter.

Contact details
For lists of all Colorado county clerks
Web: www.sos.state.co.us/pubs/elections/countyclerk.html

Other useful websites

www.colorado.gov
www.colorado.com
www.weddingsincolorado.com

 DREAM HOTEL
Hotel Jerome
330 East Main Street, Aspen, Colorado
81611, USA
Tel: 00 1 970 920 1000

Nestled in the heart of one of the world's most glamorous resorts, Hotel Jerome is a registered national landmark. It's the ideal place for active couples to tie the knot, as there are four mountains right on its doorstep offering the most superb skiing and snowboarding conditions you could wish for. It's the perfect place to snuggle up in after an energetic day on the slopes.

© Disney

Disney's Wedding Pavilion, Florida

 DREAM HOTEL
The Tides
1220 Ocean Drive, Miami Beach,
Florida 33139, USA
Tel: 00 1 305 604 5070

This hotel is an Art Deco beauty with 42 oceanfront bedrooms, three suites overlooking the ultra-hip Miami Beach and a terrace for cocktails facing legendary Ocean Drive. You're not going to find anywhere more glam for your wedding celebrations.

FLORIDA

The sunshine state of Florida has long been popular with Brits marrying abroad as it's easy to reach, offers lots of attractions and boasts a near-perfect year-round climate. Some of the more unusual places to hold your ceremony include the theme parks, such as Walt Disney World, SeaWorld and Universal Studios. Of course, the state has much more to offer than thrills and spills – there are the cosmopolitan sights and sounds of eternally hip Miami, and the haunting allure of the Everglades. The long stretches of beaches in the south are a delight and there's even the chance to get married in the water with dolphins in the Florida Keys!

Travel time
Around 9 hours 45 minutes.

Waiting period
None, but you must allow time to obtain your marriage licence.

Documents
- Valid 10-year passports.
- Birth certificates.
- Decree absolute (if divorced), marriage certificate and previous spouse's death certificate (if widowed), deed poll proof (if name changed), adoption certificate (if adopted).
- US visa or waiver form.

Minimum age
18 years without parental consent.

Further information
There is no need to apply for a licence before you arrive in Florida as they can be bought from a local courthouse on the day of the

wedding. For example, in Orlando, where most Brits go to get married, a licence currently costs US $90 (£54) and will be issued on the spot. You must both appear at the clerk's office in person, taking with you all the documents listed above and the fee. Once the application is filed, the licence is issued immediately. The process normally takes no more than 15 minutes. The licence is valid for 60 days from the date of issue.

You can only have a civil ceremony in Florida. Some of the most popular venues are the Chapel of Love, Cypress Gardens and Walt Disney World Resort (see page 180), but you can choose whatever

wedding location you desire, from 30 feet underwater at a Key Largo reef to a quiet romantic setting in a lakeside gazebo or a religious service in one of Florida's beautiful chapels.

Weather

It's not called 'the sunshine state' for nothing. The climate is sub-tropical so it is consistently warm throughout the year and can get very hot and humid in late summer. There is some risk of hurricanes in September and October.

Contact details

American Embassy
24 Grosvenor Square, London W1A 1AE
Tel: 020 7499 9000

Weddings by the Sea
PO Box 672, Sanibel Island, Florida 33957, USA
Tel: 00 1 941 472 8712
Web: www.sanibelcaptivaweddings.com

Other useful websites

www.romanticbeginnings.com

 DREAM HOTEL
Wyndham Palace Resort and Spa in the Walt Disney World Resort

1900 Buena Vista Drive, PO Box 22206
Lake Buena Vista, Florida 32830–2206, USA
Tel: 00 1 407 827 2727
Web: www.wyndhamorlandohotels.com

Wyndham Palace Resort and Spa is a fantasy paradise conveniently located inside the Walt Disney World Resort, so added extras to your stay here include free entry to all Disney theme parks, access to championship Disney golf courses and more. Universal Studios and SeaWorld are just minutes away. The bedrooms are spacious and comfy, with balconies with spectacular views and, if you need to relax before the big day, there's a European-style spa. There are several wedding locations in the grounds, including a popular lagoon setting among palm trees with a pretty fountain and bridge backdrop.

 DREAM HOTEL
Lovers Key Beach Club and Resort

8771 Estero Boulevard, Fort Myers Beach, Florida 33931, USA
Tel: 00 1 877 798 4879
E-mail: info@loverskey.com
Web: www.loverskey.com

The name says it all! This south-west Florida retreat is a haven for newlyweds and caters for small, intimate weddings and larger parties. It's situated on a small island and has white-sand beaches from where you can watch dolphins play in the sea. It also boasts a lagoon-style swimming pool with cascading waterfall that looks out over tranquil Estro Bay. The rooms have whirlpool tubs, huge beds and great views.

HAWAII

Located in the warm Pacific Ocean off America's west coast, Hawaii is a beach-lover's paradise. You can exchange your vows on one of the world's most famous stretches of sand, Waikiki Beach on Oahu. Or if you want something more unusual, how about a ceremony beneath the amazing volcanoes on Big Island or by the waterfalls on Maui? In all there are eight lush islands to choose from, including less well-known Kauai, which is considered the most beautiful and is known as the Garden Isle by the locals because of its carpet of lush green forest and fertile valleys. Big Island is, as the name suggests, the largest of the eight and is where Captain Cook first anchored his ship on discovering the islands.

 DREAM HOTEL
Four Seasons Resort Maui at Wailea

3900 Wailea Alanui, Wailea, Maui, Hawaii 96753, USA
Tel: 0800 334 6284
Web: www.fourseasons.com

There are all sorts of wedding packages at this luxury resort set on 15 acres of prime waterfront property overlooking a spectacular stretch of golden sand. Popular locations include the sculptured gardens and a grassy mound with spectacular views of the ocean at sunset. It's romance all the way at this resort, with lots of extras on offer to help you celebrate your big day, including limousine rides with champagne picnics, outdoor massages and candlelit alfresco dinners for two.

 DREAM HOTEL
The Mauna Lani Bay Hotel and Bungalows

68–1400 Mauna Lani Drive, Kohala Coast, Hawaii 96743, USA
Tel: 00 1 808 885 6622
Web: www.maunalani.com

This hotel is in a pretty pocket of the Kona Kohala Coast of Hawaii. Weddings here are intimate affairs overlooking the ocean at sunset, and there are lots of packages. The Intimate Wedding Package caters for two to 25 guests and includes marriage licence, minister, solo guitarist, bottle of champagne, two-layer wedding cake, a bouquet or fresh flower lei for the bride, boutonniere or lei for the groom and photographer. Accommodation is pretty swish, in exclusive beach bungalows with jacuzzis and round-the-clock butler service, in 15 acres of grounds where you'll see ancient fishponds that were once forbidden to all except Hawaiian royalty!

Travel time
Around 16 hours 45 minutes.

Waiting period
2 full working days may be required to process documents in some instances. There are no residency requirements.

Documents
- Valid 10-year passports.
- Copies of birth certificates.
- Decree absolute (if divorced), marriage certificate and previous spouse's death certificate (if widowed), deed poll proof (if name changed), adoption certificate (if adopted).
- US visa or waiver form.

Minimum age

18 years without parental consent. However, with written consent of both parents, legal guardian or family court, it is possible to marry as young as 15.

Further information

An application to marry must be filed with a marriage licence agent in the state (see Contact details). Both of you must appear in person before the agent – applications cannot be made by post. The licence is valid for 30 days from the date of issue, after which it will become null and void. The fee for a licence is US $60 (£36), payable in cash at the time of application.

Ceremonies can be indoors, in a church, chapel or hotel, or under the sky in a beautiful location. You can take a helicopter flight into the forest or even write your vows in the sunken remains of a ship: just about anything goes in Hawaii.

 Star choice
Film star Nicholas Cage married Lisa Marie Presley, Elvis Presley's only child, at the Mauna Lani Bay Hotel in Hawaii.

DREAM HOTEL
Hanalei Bay Resort Suites
5380 Honoiki Road, Princeville, Kauai, Hawaii 96714–0220, USA
Tel: 00 1 800 922 7866

This hotel enjoys a splendid location on the gorgeous island of Kaui, known as the Garden Isle. It's a small property, so ideal for newlyweds who want to escape the crowds, and is also the place where the song 'Some Enchanted Evening' in the classic movie *South Pacific* was filmed, so it has great pedigree for romantics! It offers a good choice of wedding packages to choose from, including indoor and outdoor venues. Hanalei is a very laid-back place – you won't find any holiday reps forcing you into excursions here, although you will find that there is a lot to do if you can bear to drag yourself away from the sunloungers. Trips arranged by the hotel include climbing soaring mountains and checking out the Ailua Falls and the Fern Grotto. On-site the hotel has lots of amenities to enjoy, including two swimming pools, a whirlpool, eight tennis courts and a vast sandy beach just a stone's throw away.

Big Island, Hawaii

Weather

Temperatures range from 16°C (60°F) to 32°C (90°C) and it is generally fine throughout the year, trade winds provide a welcome breeze from the north east.

Contact details

Hawaii Visitors' Bureau
PO Box 208, Sunbury-on-Thames,
Middlesex TW16 5RJ
Tel: 020 8941 4009
Fax: 020 8941 4011

Honolulu Marriage Licence Office
The State Health Department Building,
1250 Punchbowl Street, Honolulu, Hawaii
96813, USA
Tel: 00 1 808 586 4544

Hawaiian Island Weddings
Tel: 00 1 808 975 0350
E-mail: weddings@maui.net

Affordable Weddings of Hawaii
Tel: 00 1 808 923 4876
Fax: 00 1 808 396 0959

LAS VEGAS

In the heart of the Nevada Desert, Las Vegas is such a popular wedding destination it deserves its own special section. There's nowhere like it on earth: it's a 24-hour city where anything goes. Its biggest appeal to couples who want to marry abroad is that it is incredibly easy to wed here – you can literally step off the plane, get your licence and say 'I will'. Wedding chapels line the Strip, Las Vegas' main thoroughfare, and it's as easy as to tie the knot as it is to hire a car! Its other appeal is the string of famous couples who have fled to Vegas to get hitched throughout history, which has given the city a kitsch edge like nowhere else in the world. Where else would you be able to follow in the footsteps of such legends as Elvis and Priscilla Presley? Even modern-day Hollywood stars will turn to Las Vegas for an impromptu stroll down the aisle.

Conservatory at the Bellagio Hotel, Las Vegas

DREAM HOTEL
Four Seasons Las Vegas

3960 Las Vegas Boulevard South, Las Vegas, Nevada 89119, USA
Tel: 00 1 702 632 5000
Web: www.fourseasons.com

This establishment caused quite a stir when it opened because it is just so classy! You can get all the glitz and neon you need on the Strip, but this haven of tranquillity is the antithesis of bright lights. It also puts on some amazing weddings, with lots of locations to choose, from a balcony overlooking the fabulous pool at sunset, to the tasteful suites or landscaped gardens. Lots of extras are thrown in for a price, such as limousines, champagne and massages for two.

Travel time
Around 10 hours 30 minutes.

Waiting period
None specified.

Documents
- Valid 10-year passports.
- Birth certificates.
- Decree absolute (if divorced), marriage certificate and previous spouse's death certificate (if widowed), deed poll proof (if name changed), adoption certificate (if adopted).

♡ Star choice
You'll be following in the footsteps of the King if you get hitched in Las Vegas. Elvis Presley married Priscilla at the Aladdin Resort and Casino in 1967. Other famous nuptials to take place in the city of sin more recently include tennis aces André Agassi and Steffi Graf, and media mogul Chris Evans and singer Billie Piper.

Minimum age
18 years without parental consent. You can marry at 16 or 17 if you are accompanied by at least one of your parents or if you have an affidavit confirming your parents' permission. Proof of age will be required if you are under 21.

Further information
A marriage licence has to be obtained by the couple to be married in person from the Marriage Licence Bureau in Las Vegas (see Contact details). The office is open from 8.00 am until midnight on weekdays and from 8.00 am on Friday until midnight on Sunday every weekend. They are also open 24 hours on all holidays. The licence costs around US $50 (£30), and must be paid in cash. As soon as you've got the licence, the wedding ceremony can be conducted by any person authorised by the state of Nevada. The only proviso is that the ceremony must take place within one year of the date your licence is issued. Before you return home, you must obtain a copy of your Nevada marriage certificate as proof of your marriage. This can be purchased at the Clark County recorder's office for US $7 (£4) (see Contact details).

There are as many places to get married in Las Vegas as types of wedding ceremony. You can have anything from a short simple civil ceremony to an elaborate, romantic wedding. The simplest way to get married is by having a brief civil ceremony performed by the Las Vegas marriage commissioner, which only takes 30 minutes and will cost about US $50 (£30). Wedding chapels are a legendary part of Las Vegas and most of the casinos contain at least one wedding chapel. These chapels tend to be very elegant and grand, whereas the small independent ones are usually less elaborate. However, this means that there is something to suit all tastes. And if you don't want a traditional church ceremony, you can hold your wedding anywhere from a helicopter flying over the Las Vegas Strip to a limousine in a drive-through chapel. And then of course, there are the theme-based ceremonies – choose from thousands available, including Star Trek and Arthur and Guinevere.

Weather

Las Vegas is in the middle of a desert so it only rains for around two days out of 365! However, during the summer months the temperatures can rise to above 40°C (104°F).

Contact details

American Embassy
24 Grosvenor Square, London W1A 1AE
Tel: 020 7499 9000
Web: www.usembassy.org.uk

For your marriage licence

County Clerk's Office (Marriage Bureau)
200 South Third Street, Las Vegas, Nevada 89101, USA
Tel: 00 1 702 455 4415

For copies of marriage certificate

County Recorder's Office
PO Box 551510, Las Vegas, Nevada 89155–1510, USA
Tel: 00 1 702 455 4336

DREAM HOTEL
Bellagio Hotel
3600 Las Vegas Boulevard South,
Las Vegas, Nevada 89109, USA
Tel: 00 1 888 987 6667
E-mail:
guestservices@bellagiolasvegas.com
Web: www.bellagiolasvegas.com

This is the place to stay if you want the full-on kitsch Las Vegas, but also some serious pampering – for this is the resort that featured in hit movie *Ocean's Eleven* and at $1.6 billion is one of the most expensive hotels ever built! If you don't fancy a quick stroll down the Strip to be married by an Elvis look-alike or at a drive-in wedding tunnel, then you could choose the more sedate surroundings of the Bellagio's two wedding chapels. The large South Chapel and the more intimate East Chapel are both seriously lavish, with soft carpets you sink into, elaborate flower arrangements everywhere and lots of cream and gold furnishings. You'll be well taken care of here, with a choice of luxuries from beauty treatments on the morning of the wedding to a night in a plush suite. The hotel makes a memorable first-night honeymoon destination too, with its musical fountains and chandelier-and-gold-leaf bedecked casino – one of the few places in Vegas where guests wouldn't look out of place in a tux. In short, this place is nothing short of intoxicating.

MEXICO

Mexico might not be the first destination that springs to mind when you consider a wedding abroad, but it's rapidly becoming one of hottest places to say 'I will', and it's easy to see why this exotic destination is pulling in the crowds. As well as sand and sea, here you can visit ancient pyramids, trek through tropical jungles and shop until you drop in Mexico City. It offers a different type of holiday for every couple: if you like to be in the centre of the action, head for Cancun where the beaches are soft and white and there's always a party atmosphere. If you want to get away from it all, discover a boutique retreat on the south coast or in the lush rainforest. There's something for everyone here, and no shortage of stunning wedding destinations.

Travel time
10 hours.

Waiting period
Allow 5 working days for legal checks.

Romantic bedroom at Las Alamandas, Mexico

DREAM HOTEL
Las Alamandas
PO Box 201, San Patricio Melaque, Jalisco 48980, Mexico
Tel: 00 52 328 55000
Web: www.las-alamandas.com

Las Alamandas is Mexico's best-kept secret. It's an exquisite bolthole spread over 1,500 acres of land south of Puerto Vallarta on Mexico's Pacific Coast. If you're not on a tight budget, this is the ideal place to take over for a wedding with family and friends. If you are pulling in the purse strings a little more, then the owners are happy to arrange an intimate little ceremony in the grounds. And what beautiful grounds – full of tropical plants, colonnaded gardens and views of the nearby volcano. Its 26 suites, most situated around a courtyard, are individually decorated to a high standard in combinations of reds, fuchsias and yellows, perfectly in keeping with the exotic surroundings. Couples will want to spend time relaxing and dining on the long veranda of the main house, which has beautiful antiques, decorated ceilings and magnificent pots of colourful plants. There's also access along pretty mosaic pathways to three beaches. A simply stunning place to marry.

Documents
- Valid 10-year passports.
- Birth certificates.
- Decree absolute (if divorced), marriage certificate and previous spouse's death certificate (if widowed), deed poll proof (if name changed).
- Single status statutory declaration.

A view over the Gulf of Mexico

All documents have to be translated into Spanish by a legal translator (ask the embassy for details) and then certified by the Legalisation Department at the Foreign and Commonwealth Office in London (see below). This costs around US $30–40 (£18–24) per document plus US $30 (£18) for notarisation.

Note: A divorced woman can't marry in Mexico until one year after the divorce has been finalised.

Minimum age

18 years without parental consent. If either of you is under 18, you'll need proof of parental consent in the form of a declaration, stamped and signed by a solicitor.

Further information

Before leaving the UK, you must both attend your local register office (where a seven-day residency in the district is required) and give notice of your intention to marry. After 21 days a certificate of no impediment will be issued (this will cost £25). This certificate is only valid for three months. Once you arrive in Mexico, you will be required to undergo a local blood and HIV test. This is

DREAM HOTEL
La Casa que Canta
Zihuatanejo Bay, Guerrero 40880, Mexico
Tel: 00 52 755 555 7000
E-mail: info@lacasaquecanca.com
Web: www.casaquecanta.com

There are lots of romantic places to wed at this unusual hotel on Mexico's Pacific Coast. One of the most popular choices is to exchange your wedding vows on the wooden deck by La Casa que Canta's spectacular 'infinity' pool as the sun sets. Or you could get a little bit closer to nature and say 'I will' on the deck of the resort's saltwater pool, which is carved into the cliffs just a few feet above the crashing waves on Zihuatanejo Bay. Once you're married, it makes a splendid choice for a honeymoon too. Set on a promontory overlooking the bay, it's a multi-tiered resort set in rocky cliffs. The open architectural design – it's constructed without glass or metal – allows the warm Mexican breezes to operate as a delightful air-conditioning system in your bedrooms. There are just 24 suites and while the thatch-roofed accommodations aren't plush, they are romantic and elegant. Fixtures include hand-crafted furniture, sculptures and pottery. It's the little extras that make this place special, particularly the turn-down service, when housekeepers carry baskets overflowing with fragrant flower petals to guest rooms each evening and decorate bedspreads with enchanting floral designs.

In Mexico only civil marriages are recognised as legal. You may have a religious ceremony but it will have no legal validity anywhere. A civil wedding in Mexico is fully valid for legal purposes worldwide. **Note:** The ceremony will be conducted in Spanish in the presence of an interpreter and the marriage certificate issued will also be in Spanish.

Weather

It's consistently warm, with temperatures always above 21°C (70°F). The rainy season runs from June to October.

Contact details

Mexican Tourist Office
Wakefield House, 41 Trinity Square, London EC3N 4DJ
Tel: 020 7488 9392

Mexican Embassy
42 Hertford Street, London W1Y 7TF
Tel: 020 7499 8586

Mexican Consulate
8 Halkin Street, London SW1X 7DW
Tel: 020 7235 6393
Fax: 020 7235 5480
E-mail: consullondon@easynet.co.uk

Legalisation Department
Foreign and Commonwealth Office, 20 Victoria Street, London SW1H 0NZ
Tel: 020 7210 2520/1/2/3
Web: www.fco.gov.uk

Useful websites

www.mexiconline.com

⋆♡ **Star choice**
Film stars Sarah Michelle Gellar (of Buffy the Vampire Slayer *fame) and Freddie Prinze Junior flew to Mexico to wed there in 2002.*

compulsory and costs US $120–160 (£72–96) per couple. The Civil Registrar's Office will recommend a doctor or clinic.

NEW YORK

The most popular place for Brits to wed in New York State is, of course, Manhattan. It's clear to see why: with stunning backdrops such as the Statue of Liberty and Empire State Building you'd be hard-pushed to find a more exciting and beautiful city wedding location in the world. It's the ideal destination for couples who want a cosmopolitan city destination rather than a barefoot beach ceremony. New York has a vibrant, sophisticated vibe that is hard to beat, and it's also home to some of the best shops in the world, so be sure to take your credit card! It will also make an ideal wedding location to complement a honeymoon in the Caribbean or on the West Coast.

Travel time
Around 8 hours.

Waiting period
24 hours.

Documents
- Valid 10-year passports.
- Decree absolute (if divorced), marriage certificate and previous spouse's death certificate (if widowed).

Minimum age
18 years without parental consent. If either of you is 16 or 17 years of age, you must present written proof of consent of both parents.

Further information
A couple who intend to be married in New York State must apply in person for a marriage licence to any town or city clerk in the state. The application for a licence must be

 DREAM HOTEL
The Plaza
Fifth Avenue at Central Park South, New York, NY 10019, USA
Tel: 00 1 212 759 3000
Fax: 00 1 212 759 3167
E-mail: newyork@fairmont.com
Web: www.fairmont.com

The crown jewel of Manhattan's fabled Fifth Avenue, The Plaza reigns over New York with a grace and glamour that has drawn visitors from around the globe for over 100 years. Its location on the edge of Central Park has something to do with its allure, as does its château-like façade, which stands out amongst the skyscrapers. Inside, it's a homage to a bygone era: chandeliers glint, the polished floors dazzle and afternoon tea is served in the elegant lounge. From glorious meeting rooms and palatial ballrooms to the brilliance of the legendary restaurants, The Plaza is the ultimate venue in New York to stage a glitzy wedding. If you've got a big budget, the hotel can arrange small or large parties and the staff will cater to literally your every whim – at a price!

The most famous wedding to take place at The Plaza in recent years is that of film stars Michael Douglas and Catherine Zeta Jones. Eddie Murphy also exchanged vows here, as did millionaire businessman Donald Trump.

signed by both parties in the presence of the town or city clerk. If the marriage licence is issued outside New York City (but still in New York State), the licence fee costs US $25 (£15). If it is issued by the city clerk of the City of New York (see Contact details), it costs

DREAM HOTEL
Waldorf-Astoria
301 Park Avenue, New York, NY 10022, USA
Tel: 00 1 212 355 3000

The world-renowned Waldorf-Astoria is located in the heart of Midtown Manhattan and is within walking distance of the theatre district, as well as the shopping areas and art galleries on Madison and Fifth Avenue. This Art Deco hotel is well known for its glamorous weddings; it can cater for everything from tiny gatherings right up to 1,000-plus guests in the Grand Ballroom, which rises four floors and boasts a 10-foot-wide crystal chandelier.

US president John F Kennedy and his wife Jackie Bouvier spent their wedding night at the Waldorf.

$30 (£18). Once the couple have been married, the officiant who performed the marriage ceremony will return the completed licence to the issuing clerk, who will, within 15 days, send the couple a certificate of marriage registration. If you do not receive this certificate within four weeks of your wedding, you should contact the town or city clerk who issued the licence. A licence is valid for 60 days.

Some couples have a civil ceremony performed while preparing or waiting for a religious

New York skyline

ceremony. The officiant of the subsequent religious ceremony may require that a licence be presented before performing the ceremony. In that case a couple already legally married may apply for a second or subsequent licence.

Weather
Similar to the UK, although a little more extreme. The city can feel very hot and oppressive in the summer and it can snow heavily at times between December and February.

Contact details
City Clerk of New York (Manhattan) Municipal Building, 1 Centre Street, New York, NY10007, USA
Tel: 00 1 212 669 2400

For general information
NYC and Company
Tel: 020 7202 6368
Web: www.nycvisit.com

DREAM HOTEL
The Mark
Madison Avenue at East 77th Street, New York, NY 10021, USA
Tel: 00 1 212 744 4300
Web: www.mandarinoriental.com

One of Manhattan's finest hotels, The Mark is tucked away on the exclusive Upper East Side and is very romantic in an elegant and understated way. Its rooms are fabulously furnished with king-size beds, comfy sofas, marble bath tubs and flowers, and there are lots of extra luxuries like Molton Brown toiletries and decanters of bath crystals to enjoy. It's also famous for its restaurant and function suites – perfect for a wedding reception – and its bar, where you could spot familiar faces such as Julia Roberts.

WASHINGTON DC

Not to be confused with
Washington State (see page 160), the
city of Washington DC (short for
Dulles County) is situated on the
East Coast of the United States. It's
not an obvious choice as a place for
Brits to marry abroad, but is
certainly one of the most original.
The ideal marriage venues in the
USA's capital are its famous hotels,
which have attracted politicians and
actors throughout the years. In
terms of a honeymoon destination,
there's lots to see and do, from the
famous landmarks, such as the
White House and Pentagon, to the
wonderful architecture and world-
class restaurants and sophisticated
bars.

Travel time
Around 8 hours 30 minutes.

Waiting period
5 working days.

Documents
- Valid 10-year passports.
- Birth certificates.
- Decree absolute (if divorced),
  marriage certificate and previous
  spouse's death certificate
  (if widowed).

Minimum age
18 years without parental consent.
16 years, with parental consent,
which has to be provided in person
or by a notarised letter.

Further information
To apply for a marriage licence, you
must both appear in person. The
licence, which must be bought in
cash and costs around US $45 (£27),
is valid indefinitely, so you can take
as long as you like before marrying.

Marriage licences are addressed
to the minister who will perform the
ceremony, so you must arrange this
beforehand. After the ceremony, the
minister has to complete the

The Capitol Building, Washington DC

marriage certificate for the bride and groom and then return another certificate to the clerk of the District of Columbia Court of General Sessions within ten days of the marriage.

Weather

Summer temperatures are 21–26° (70–80°F) but it can feel much hotter in the city. Winter temperatures frequently drop below freezing, with occasional heavy snowfall.

Contact details

Washington DC CVA
c/o Representation Plus, 11 Baldes Court, 121 Deodar Road, London SW15 2NU
Tel: 020 8877 4521

 DREAM HOTEL
ANA Hotel
2401 M Street NW, Washington DC 20037, USA
Tel: 0800 262 4683

Couples in love will adore this majestic hotel, the most famous in the state, which has played host to everyone from presidents to film stars. Recent visitors include Demi Moore, Eddie Murphy and Susan Sarandon, and it's well known as a place that hosts intimate weddings with a difference – *Batman* star Chris O'Donnell celebrated his wedding here. The location is superb for outdoor weddings in the Colonnade Garden Courtyard, which features a three-tiered Italian fountain in its centre and for large parties the Grand Ballroom is particularly impressive. The hotel is situated in the city's fashionable West End and is a great base from which to explore the famous landmarks, such as the White House and Kennedy Centre.

WASHINGTON STATE

Washington State is a great wedding location if you're looking for somewhere less obvious and off the beaten track. Confusingly, it's just about as far as it's possible to be from Washington DC, on the opposite coast of the United States. Washington is known as the Evergreen State and is bounded on the north by the beautiful Canadian province of British Columbia, on the east by Idaho, on the south by Oregon, and on the west by the Pacific Ocean. There are lots of islands to explore in the series of channels in the north west, including the Strait of Juan de Fuca, Haro Strait and the Strait of Georgia, and the magnificent Columbia River is also worth checking out. Tourism in the state has grown considerably in recently years as people flock to see the wonderful scenery and native flora and fauna, which exist in abundance.

Travel time

Approximately 9 hours.

Waiting period

No residency requirements but the licence has a 3-day waiting period.

Documents

- Valid 10-year passports.
- Birth certificates.
- Decree absolute (if divorced).

Minimum age

18 years without parental consent. If aged between 17 and 18 you need to have a parent (or legal guardian) present with you to provide their consent.

Dream hotel
Kiana Lodge

14976 Sandy Hook Road NE, Poulsbo,
Washington 98370, USA
Tel: 00 1 206 282 4633
Fax: 00 1 360 598 4311
Web: www.kianalodge.com

Kiana Lodge can be considered a true taste of the beauty of the Pacific North-west. Located 50 minutes from the Seattle waterfront, and reached via a 35-minute ferry ride plus 10–15 minutes of driving, the lodge is surrounded by fragrant cedars, tall firs and many varieties of rhododendrons. Kiana is situated on 1,000 feet of waterfront and six acres of beautiful gardens. The manicured grounds are ablaze with spectacular colour from early spring to late autumn and the rustic elegance of the lodge is a perfect place for a beautiful indoor wedding.

Further information

You can obtain your marriage licence, which costs around US $52 (£31), by applying either in person (only one of the couple need go) or by mail. A licence is valid for 60 days. You should order certified copies of your marriage licence after the wedding (when applying you will receive written instructions on how to do this). The certified copies will prove your legal marriage to other jurisdictions.

Under Washington State law, any minister or priest of any church or religious denomination, and any Washington State judge or justice (practising or retired) can perform a marriage ceremony. There are lots of popular locations to marry, but it is worth booking well in advance,

particularly if you want a summer wedding date.

Weather

The warm weather season for Seattle and the state of Washington is May through July, when temperatures are around 18–20°C (65–68°F). It can rain heavily at any time.

Contact details

Seattle Convention and Visitors' Bureau
1 Convention Place, 701 Pike Street, Suite 800, Seattle, Washington 98101, USA
Tel: 00 1 206 461 5840
www.seeseattle.org

Dream hotel
Salish Lodge and Spa

6501 Railroad Avenue, PO Box 1109
Snoqualmie, Washington 98065–1109, USA
Tel: 00 1 425 888 2556
Fax: 00 1 425 888 2533
E-mail: reservations@salishlodge.com

One of the most romantic of all Seattle hotels, the Salish Lodge offers an elegantly rustic setting for weddings, honeymoons and long weekend getaways. There's the opportunity to enjoy exquisite dining, a blissful spa, exceptional facilities and breathtaking scenery. Perched at the crest of the magnificent 268-foot Snoqualmie Falls, the hotel offers a unique combination of comfort and style. It's also perfectly situated for visiting the surrounding area, being located 35 minutes from downtown Seattle and the Snoqualmie Pass summit, within 40 minutes of Sea-Tac International Airport and just three hours from Vancouver in neighbouring British Columbia and Portland, Oregon.

Washington State

 DREAM HOTEL
The Woodmark Hotel
1200 Carillon Point, Kirkland,
Washington 98033, USA
Tel: 00 1 425 822 3700
Fax: 00 1 425 822 3699
E-mail: mail@thewoodmark.com

Situated by Lake Washington just outside Seattle, The Woodmark is a very romantic Washington hotel, and therefore popular for weddings and honeymooners. The 100-room hotel has great views of the lake and mountains, and the rooms have roaring fires, marble bathrooms and lots of overstuffed sofas to cuddle up on. Famous faces through the door include Paul McCartney and actress Cynthia Geary from *Northern Exposure*.

Useful websites
www.ci.seattle.wa.us/
www.bridesandgrooms.com/links/wa.html

To request a marriage ceremony
www.cityofseattle.net/courts/judmag/
marriageRequest.htm

To download a copy of the marriage licence application form
www.metrokc.gov/lars/marriage/index.htm

CHAPTER 10

CANADA

Canada is famous for its variety of wildlife and spectacular scenery, panoramic lakes, majestic mountains, wide-open prairies and, of course, the Niagara Falls. However, there is another more sophisticated side to this immense country, which newlyweds will want to check out, including the cosmopolitan cities of Montreal, Toronto and Quebec, with their fabulous restaurants, five-star hotels and stunning architecture.

Canada is also a fun place to visit at any time of the year. In the summer you can hike through the vast national parks, visit the coast and explore the tranquil lakes. The winters bring a heavy blanket of snow, providing some of the best skiing and snowboarding conditions in the world, not to mention a highly romantic backdrop for your wedding!

HEALTH TIPS

- The only health risk to visitors to Canada is rabies, but post-exposure treatment is usually readily available.
- Do make sure you take out comprehensive medical insurance, as bills here can really mount up.

ALBERTA

Home of the Canadian Rockies and some of the best hotels in Canada, Alberta is a must for couples looking for the ultimate scenic backdrop for their wedding. Other attractions include hot springs to wallow in, stunning lakes, helicopter tours and, in winter, skiing and sleigh rides.

Travel time

Around 10 hours.

Waiting period

None specified.

 DREAM HOTEL
The Fairmont Chateau Lake Louise

111 Lake Louise Drive, Lake Louise, Alberta, Canada T0L 1E0
Tel: 00 1 403 522 3511
E-mail: chateaulakelouise@fairmont.com
Web: www.fairmont.com

Step through the doors at The Fairmont Chateau Lake Louise and you enter a truly romantic Rocky Mountain retreat. Although this is a year-round sanctuary, the best time to go is the winter when you can indulge in fondue dinners, sleigh rides through the forest and hot toddies by the roaring fires. It's also the best time to travel there if you want a 'white' wedding, or simply a honeymoon that includes lots of snow sports. The hotel offers a 'Love and Hugs' romance package in the winter, which includes a cosy room, breakfast in bed and a surprise gift. Other reasons to visit are the excellent Canadian cuisine and the wealth of activities on offer, including canoeing, hiking, skating and skiing, all in glorious surroundings.

Documents

- Valid 10-year passports.
- Birth certificates with both parents' names.
- Decree absolute (if divorced), marriage certificate and previous spouse's death certificate (if widowed), adoption certificate (if adopted), deed poll proof (if name changed).

Minimum age

18 years without parental consent. If either of you is under 18, written proof of parental consent is required.

Further information

Prior to getting married, couples have to apply in person for a marriage licence at a register office in the province of Alberta. The

---

DREAM HOTEL
Fairmont Banff Springs

PO Box 960, Banff, Alberta, Canada T1L 1J4
Tel: 00 1 403 762 2211
E-mail: banffsprings@fairmont.com
Web: www.fairmont.com

Few hotels in the world can rival the majesty, hospitality and scenery of this fabulous establishment. Its unique blend of opulence and seclusion has been a symbol of Rocky Mountain magnificence for more than a century. Styled after a Scottish baronial castle, The Fairmont Banff Springs offers stunning vistas, championship golf courses, unparalleled skiing and classic cuisine, as well as the Willow Stream, a world-class European-style spa. Weddings can be arranged on an individual basis.

licence is valid for three months from the date of issue and costs around CA $40 (£18).

You can have either a religious or civil ceremony in Alberta. Civil services are performed by a marriage commissioner and popular settings to choose from include Bow Falls, Hoodoo Lookout and Vermilion Lake overlooking Victoria Glacier by Lake Louise.

Weather
The winter months are very snowy and cold, summer months warm and dry.

Contact details
Government Services, Alberta Registries
Box 2023, Edmonton, Alberta, Canada
T5J 4W7
Tel: 00 1 780 427 7013
Web:
www.gov.ab.ca/gs/information/vs/contact/cfm

BRITISH COLUMBIA
British Columbia is arguably Canada's most beautiful province and it certainly offers some of the most stunning scenery in the world. There are lush green forests to explore, soaring mountains capped with snow, rivers for white-water rafting and canoeing, and vast stretches of unspoilt beach. It's also home to Vancouver, a cosmopolitan city with lots to offer in terms of sightseeing and entertainment. Whether you fancy getting hitched at the top of a mountain or by the edge of the ocean, you'll be spoilt for wedding locations in BC.

Travel time
Around 9 hours.

DREAM HOTEL
Chateau Whistler Resort
4600 Chateau Boulevard, Whistler, British Columbia, Canada V0N 1B4
Tel: 00 1 604 966 3092
Web: www.fairmont.com

Located at the bottom of the stunning Blackcomb Mountain, this resort is as good as it gets if you're winter sports enthusiasts. Right on your doorstep are some of the best skiing conditions in the world, so if you want a 'white' wedding with some action thrown in you're going to want to head here to exchange vows. If you need any added enticement, it's got one of North America's best spas and from its restaurant to its comfortable, elegant rooms, this place oozes five-star luxury. It's also just steps from the many restaurants, cafes, boutiques and fun nightclubs of Whistler.

Whistler, British Columbia

Waiting period

None once you have a marriage licence.

Documents

- Valid 10-year passport or other identification showing your full name; place and date of birth; evidence of marital status; current address.
- Decree absolute if either party is recently divorced (within 31 days). No licence may be issued until a divorce has been finalised by the courts.

Minimum age

19 years without parental consent.

Further information

The marriage licence costs around CA $75 (£33). The fee must be paid at the time of the application – the licence will be issued immediately and is valid for three months. You must apply in person at the local municipal office or city hall for the town or area you wish to get married in.

Note: Only one member of the couple needs to apply but identification documents (see above) must be provided for both.

Couples can choose a religious or civil ceremony. Whichever you choose, it must be witnessed by two people. Religious ceremonies are performed by a religious representative of your choice, civil ceremonies by marriage commissioners. The religious representative or marriage commissioner who performs the wedding ceremony will help you to complete the necessary marriage registration form and is required, under the Marriage Act, to send it within 48 hours of the ceremony to the Vital Statistics Agency, where the marriage is registered and a legal record is kept.

Weather
British Columbia is a year-round destination with four distinct seasons. In winter, from late November to March, or April in the mountains, there is snow on the ground in most parts except the south-west corner, including Vancouver and Victoria. Spring comes early to this area. Summer typically runs from June to September.

Contact details
British Columbia Division of Vital Statistics Ministry of Health
818 Fort Street, Victoria, British Columbia, Canada V8W 1H8
Tel: 00 1 800 663 8328
Web: www.htlh.gov.bc.ca/vs

DREAM HOTEL
Long Beach Lodge Resort
PO Box 897, Tofino, British Columbia, Canada V0R 2Z0
Tel: 00 1 877 844 7873
E-mail: lbl@island.net
Web: www.longbeachlodgeresort.com

For a seriously romantic wedding location and honeymoon spot, consider Long Beach Lodge Resort, a luxurious beachfront resort perched on the edge of Cox Bay, between the pristine beauty of the Pacific Rim National Park and spectacular Clayoquot Sound. This cedar-shingled lodge offers first-class amenities and service in a relaxed setting.

For general information
Visit Canada
PO Box 5396, Northampton NN1 2FA
Tel: 0906 871 5000 (calls charged at premium rate – 60p/min)
E-mail: visitcanada@dialpipex.com
Web: www.travelcanada.ca

For information on Whistler
www.mywhistler.com

Niagara Falls, Ontario

ONTARIO

This vast state is so large you'll need to spend a month here if you want to really see all the sites! For a city wedding destination there's the cultural melting-pot of Toronto, Canada's largest city, which sits on the edge of Lake Ontario. If you're after something a little more unusual, then head for Niagara Falls, where you can exchange vows and then take a helicopter flight over the top of the natural wonder or even join a trail into the hidden caves behind the waterfalls.

Travel time
Around 8 hours.

Waiting period
None specified.

Documents
- Valid 10-year passports.
- Birth certificates.
- Decree absolute or certificate of annulment (if previously married). See below.

A divorcee whose former marriage was dissolved or annulled in a place other than Canada must obtain authorisation from the Ontario Minister of Consumer and Commercial Relations before a marriage licence can be issued. To obtain this authorisation, the applicants or a lawyer representing them must submit the following to the office of the Registrar General:
- A completed marriage licence application signed by both applicants.
- A copy of the decree of divorce or annulment (certified by the proper court officer in the jurisdiction the divorce/

annulment was granted) sealed by the court, together with a certified translation if the decree is in a language other than English or French.
- A statement of sole responsibility for each divorce signed by both applicants (blank affidavits are available from the local issuer of marriage licences).
- A letter from an Ontario lawyer, addressed to both applicants, giving legal reasons why the divorce or annulment should be recognised in the Province of Ontario.

Minimum age
18 years without parental consent.

Further information
A licence to marry may be obtained from the municipal clerk's office. Only one of the couple need appear in person, but the application must be signed by both applicants. The issuer may require proof of age of both parties, so if only one party is appearing in person, he/she must bring proof of age of the other party. The marriage licence is valid for use anywhere in Ontario. It expires three months after the date of issue.

It is possible to have a religious or civil ceremony in Ontario. The most popular place to tie the knot is, of course, Niagara Falls, although be warned, you can't get married right by the famous waterfall. The closest you can get is the Oakes Garden Theatre (see Contact details), a beautiful spot with a dramatic view of the falls in the background. You must also arrange for two witnesses to be present at the ceremony.

Weather

Very cold in winter, so unsuitable for outdoor weddings. Summers are bright and warm.

Contact details

Office of the Registrar General
Box 4600, 189 Red River Road, Thunder Bay, Ontario, Canada ONP7B 6L8
Tel: 00 1 416 325 8305
Web: www.ccr.gov.on.ca/mccr/orgindex.htm

Oakes Garden
Niagara Park
Tel: 00 1 877 642 7275

 DREAM HOTEL
Niagara Falls Marriott Fallsview
6740 Fallsview Boulevard, Niagara Falls, Ontario, Canada L2G3W6

Located just 100 yards from the edge of Niagara, in the heart of the tourist district, this is a great place to stay if you want to hold your wedding by the falls. The hotel is built in a stunning curved shape and has specially designed windows, so that you can see the waterfalls from pretty much every one of the 427 well-appointed bedrooms. Additional amenities include a universal gym with fitness equipment, indoor pool, two whirlpools, a sauna, steam room and spa, outdoor sun deck and casino shuttle.

CHAPTER 11

SOUTH AMERICA

The sizzling cities, golden beaches and lush jungles of South America make it an exciting destination. This is a continent so blessed with natural wonders, spectacular wildlife and breathtaking sights that those who visit are usually hooked for life. Among the hundreds of things to see and do, top of the list has to be a trip to the tropical Amazon jungle. Other must-dos include trekking in the mountains of the Andes, sailing across Lake Titicaca, navigating the Inca trail and dancing to the lively rhythms of the carnival in Rio de Janeiro. Peru, in particular, is an exciting place to head for – you can say your vows in the capital, Lima, and then head to Machu Picchu to watch the sun rise – one of the most romantic experiences in the world!

HEALTH TIPS

- You will be advised to have inoculations against hepatitis A, typhoid and possibly yellow fever, depending on what areas you wish to visit in South America, as well as diphtheria, tuberculosis, rabies and hepatitis B.
- Low-lying areas may also carry a risk of malaria, although this is not common west of the Andes. Check with your doctor or practice nurse to see what you require.

BRAZIL

Brazil is exotic, colourful and
completely unique. From
cosmopolitan Rio de Janiero, with
its lively carnivals and fabulous bars
and restaurants, to the golden sands
of Copacabana Beach, not
forgetting the vast expanses of
tropical rainforest in the interior,
this huge country provides a wealth
of exciting places to go, sizzling
sights to see and dramatic locations
for your wedding ceremony.

Travel time
Around 13 hours.

Waiting period
5 working days.

Documents
- Valid 10-year passports.
- Birth certificates (originals,
  showing names of both parents).
- Decrees nisi and absolute and
  original marriage certificate (if
  divorced), originals of marriage
  certificate and previous spouse's
  death certificate (if widowed).
- Certificate of no impediment.
  This can be offered either as a

**Dream hotel
SuperClubs Breezes Costa
do Sauipe**

Tel: 00 1 954 925 0925
Fax: 00 1 954 925 0334
E-mail: info@superclubs.com
Web: www.superclubs.com

A fun resort, located 50 miles
north of the city of Salvador in
the State of Bahia, Brazil. As well as
the sun, sand and fabulous facilities,
the other big attraction is that the
hotel offers a free wedding
arrangement service. If you're
tempted, it does require three weeks'
notice to complete the formalities as
all the documents need to be sent to
the local Brazilian Embassy to be
legalised. After legalisation, the
documents must be sent to
SuperClubs Breezes Costa do Sauipe
at least one month before the
wedding.

You need to arrive at Breezes five
days before the ceremony to sign the
documents. However, once you've
sorted out the initial paperwork, you
can relax and let the hotel staff take
responsibility for everything else,
such as the ceremony and marriage
certificate.

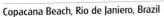

Copacana Beach, Rio de Janiero, Brazil

172

BRAZIL

non-impediment certificate issued by your local register office in the UK or as a notarised affidavit, signed by two persons over 21 years of age, declaring that they have known the applicant for more than two years, and that to their knowledge there is no impediment to his/her marriage.

- A certificate of residence for each of you. This may be presented either in the form of a declaration issued by your local electoral register office in the UK, stating your address according to their archives for the last two years, or as a notarised affidavit stating where you have been living for the past two years.
- A power of attorney, drawn up by a notary and legalised by the Brazilian Consulate, when required by the register office in Brazil.

Minimum age
21 years without parental consent.

DREAM HOTEL
Copacabana Palace
Avenida Atlantica, 1702, 22021–001
Rio de Janeiro, Brazil
Tel: 00 55 21 2548 7070

Its superb location on Copacabana Beach makes this a firm favourite for weddings, as well as the fact that it's one of the grandest hotels in South America. Anyone who is anyone has been here, from artists and royalty to Hollywood stars. It's got some of the best restaurants in South America too, such as the Cipriani, which serves a wonderful selection of Italian delicacies.

Further information
All documents issued in the United Kingdom must be legalised by the Brazilian Consulate General in London. All documents must be translated into Portuguese by an authorised translator, preferably in Brazil (Brazilian Portuguese is not the same as the Portuguese spoken in Portugal!) The consular fee is £16 per document.

Weather
In a tropical zone, with temperatures averaging 26°C (80°F), Brazil can be exceptionally hot and humid in parts, although the coastal areas are usually more moderate. It can be cooler in the winter months of July to August.

Contact details
Brazilian Consulate General
6 St Alban's Street, London SW1Y 4SQ
Tel: 020 7930 9055
Fax: 020 7839 8958
E-mail: consulado@cgbrasil.org.uk
(Open to the public Monday to Friday, 10.00 am to 4.00 pm)

Foreign and Commonwealth Office Legalisation Department, 20 Victoria Street, London SW1H 0NZ
Tel: 020 7210 2520/1/2/3
Web: www.fco.gov.uk

PERU

Couples who want a truly unique destination steeped in culture and history will want to head to Peru for their wedding day, although you should be warned, making the arrangements can be quite a complicated process! It's a fabulous place for a cultural honeymoon too – you can wander around colonial cities that have preserved the legacy of Spanish invaders, visit the ancient Inca capital of Cuzco and explore the lost city of Machu Picchu.

The Amazon Basin, which occupies half of Peru, is one of the world's Top Ten biodiversity 'hot spots' and the coastal desert areas, with their huge rolling dunes and fishing villages, are a scenic wonder. But you don't have to be a zoologist, an anthropologist or a mountain climber to enjoy Peru: all you need is a keen eye, a love of landscape and an interest in history. I should perhaps add that petty crime is rife, but there is no reason why you should let that deter you as long as you take sensible precautions, such as having a very secure money belt.

Travel time
Around 14 hours.

Waiting period
Non specified.

Documents
- Valid 10-year passports.
- Birth certificates, legalised by the Foreign and Commonwealth Office and the Peruvian Consular General.
- Results of recent blood tests (including AIDS) and lung tests – you'll need a certificate issued by a GP or laboratory in Peru no more than 30 days before wedding.
- 1 photograph of the prospective bride and groom, together.
- Receipt for the marriage fees from the *Oficina de Recaudación de Rentas* (fee-collection office) in Peru.
- Consular certificate of non-impediment of marriage, translated into Spanish, legalised first by the consulate of your country of origin and then by the Peruvian Ministry of Foreign Affairs. Alternatively, you can present a certificate of non-impediment of marriage issued by your town hall in the UK and legalised first by the Foreign and Commonwealth Office (see Contact details) and then by the Peruvian consulate in the UK. Some registrars will accept an affidavit, which needs to be legalised by the Peruvian consulate if prepared in the UK.

Further information
All documents bearing the signature and stamp of the Peruvian Consulate General must be legalised by the *Direccion de Documentacio* (director of documentation) at the Peruvian Ministry of Foreign Affairs in Lima. It is advisable to ask the register office in Peru where you intend to get married whether or not they require any other documents.

Minimum age
18 years without parental consent.

Weather
The only thing predictable about Peru's weather is its unpredictability.

Generally speaking it has two seasons, wet and dry. In the highlands, the dry season is from June to October with an average temperature of 20°C (68°F). The Amazon basin experiences high average daytime temperatures, while nights tend to be much cooler. The desert coast is arid. From January to March the sky is clear and the air tends to be sticky and hot, around 27°C (80°F), but it can get much hotter.

Contact details

Embassy of Peru
52 Sloane Street, London SW1X 9SP
Tel: 020 7235 1917
E-mail: postmaster@peruembassy-uk.com
Web: www.peruembassy-uk.com

Peruvian Consulate
Tel: 020 7838 9223
E-mail: consulate@peruembassy-uk.com

DREAM HOTEL
Hotel Monasterio
Calle Palacios 136, Plazoleta Nazarenas, Cusco, Peru
Tel: 00 51 84 241 777
Web: www.hotelmonasterio.com.ar

The exquisite Hotel Monasterio was once the hallowed San Antonio Abad Seminary, which was built more than 300 years ago by the Spanish, and is now considered one of the most romantic places in Peru. While providing you with the comforts and quality of a modern five-star hotel, its main attraction is that it's also a museum! Here you're literally surrounded by ancient artifacts, architecture and paintings straight from Cusco's Inca and Spanish culture. If you fancy marrying in this historic wonder, there's a chapel in the grounds, and you can book a package that includes a photo tour of Machu Picchu after the ceremony. Wedding receptions are usually held in the hotel's Tupay restaurant.

Machu Picchu, Peru

CHAPTER 12
UNUSUAL PLACES TO MARRY

For most people, the words 'getting married abroad' immediately bring images of golden, palm-fringed beaches to mind, but there is a wealth of other possibilities for you to consider. This chapter is dedicated to bringing you some unconventional ideas for getting married in some of the world's most extraordinary places. Whether it's exchanging vows at the top of a ski slope or in a hot-air balloon as the sun rises over Las Vegas or tying the knot at a hotel made from ice in Canada, you're sure to find a dream destinations in this section to really fire your imagination.

For information about marriage arrangements and the documents you'll need in each country, refer to the previous chapters.

The Grand Canyon, Arizona, USA

UP IN THE AIR

Some couples aren't content to keep their feet on the ground when it comes to their wedding day. If you want to combine your ceremony with the exhilaration of flying through the air, here is a selection of choices for take-off.

Hot-air balloon over Las Vegas

The happy couple must obtain their marriage licence beforehand. On their wedding day, a limousine will pick up the bride and groom and take them to the launching site for the wedding. After the ceremony, they will be transported by limousine back to the hotel. Package includes balloon with pilot and crew, minister, Love Recipe and Rules for a Happy Marriage!
Cost: US $1,000 (£600)

Contact
Little White Chapel in the Sky
1301 Las Vegas Boulevard South,
Las Vegas, Nevada 89104, USA
Tel: 00 1 702 382 5943
Web: www.alittlewhitechapel.com

Helicopter over
the Grand Canyon

Your wedding day begins with a private limousine transfer from your hotel to the private helicopter that awaits your arrival. Embark on an unforgettable, narrated flight in complete luxury from Las Vegas to the floor of the Grand Canyon. You will actually descend 4,000 feet into the depths of the canyon, past sheer rock formations before touching down by the banks of the historic Colorado River. Exchange your vows with the one you love in the amazing Grand Canyon, then celebrate with a champagne toast and a wedding cake. As a grande finale, you will fly down the Las Vegas Strip ready to enjoy the city that never sleeps, to your limousine, which will spirit you back to your hotel.
Cost: US $2,449 (£1,472)

Contact
Grand Canyon Tour Company
Tel: 0800 9175156
E-mail:
salesdesk@grandcanyontourcompany.com
Web: www.grandcanyontourcompany.com

Hot-air balloon over mountains
in New Zealand

For a truly magical experience, try flying in a hot-air balloon over the city of Christchurch and the snow-capped mountains in New Zealand's South Island. Exchange your vows in the sky, then celebrate with a glass of champagne when you're back on terra firma. The flight does depend on good weather, and mornings tend to be the best time for good flying conditions. Your hot-air balloon civil ceremony package for a couple without guests includes your New Zealand marriage licence, arrangement and application fee, plus exclusive use of a six-passenger hot-air balloon for your ceremony and a one-hour balloon flight. You will also be given a fresh floral bouquet for the bride and matching buttonhole for the groom. The organisers will also arrange for two witnesses as required by New Zealand law, bridal car transfers from centrally located accommodation to your take-off site, a bottle of sparkling wine for a post-ceremony toast, a hot-air balloon certificate and a professional wedding photographer who will take 72 shots in 35mm format colour film. The film is processed, printed and the photos arranged in a quality flip-style album – and couples get to keep all negatives.

Cost: NZ $5,659 (£1,961)

Contact

NZ Wedding Services Ltd
PO Box 14037, Christchurch, New Zealand
Tel: 00 64 3 359 8160 or 00 64 3 359 3993
Fax: 00 64 3 359 3998
E-mail: info@nzweddingservices.co.nz
Web: www.nzweddingservices.co.nz

African hot-air balloon safari

Sail off into the golden early morning light of the Masai Mara Game Reserve, to exchange your vows at sunrise, whilst flying in a specially decorated hot-air balloon over herds of game. Then, after a sumptuous champagne breakfast followed by a game drive, you'll go back to your tent to celebrate again with a romantic candlelit dinner on the veranda of your tented suite. The package includes transportation and the services of the wedding registrar, the marriage licence and certificate, a wedding cake for up to six persons, bouquet and buttonhole for the bride and groom and a small wedding gift.

Cost: US $1,450 (£872) per couple (does not include accommodation)

Contact

Wild Destinations Limited
7th Floor Standard Building, Wabera Street,
PO Box 44159, 00100 GPO Nairobi, Kenya
Tel: 00 254 2 240559/247223
E-mail: wld.dest@africaonline.co.ke

IN, ON AND UNDER THE WATER

If you'd prefer to be out on the ocean waves, or even in them, rather than standing on a sandy beach, then these unusual water weddings are for you. These days there is lots of choice available, from classic ceremonies performed on board gleaming white yachts, to swimming with dolphins and even diving to the depths of the ocean to exchange vows. Whatever you choose, it's sure to be a memorable day!

On a Malaysian luxury yacht

Exchange your vows with the one you love on board the *YTL Lady*, a 64-foot luxury yacht, moored off Pangkor Laut in Malaysia, one of the most beautiful islands in the world! Whether you hire it just for the two of you or take along your friends and family (maximum 18 passengers), this is an ideal way to celebrate your special day in style.

Cost: On application

Contact

Pangkor Laut Resort
Tel: 0800 9899 9999
Web: www.pangkorlautresort.com

Underwater wedding in the US Virgin Islands

What about saying 'I will' underwater amidst a coral reef off the beautiful island of St John's, which is a world-renowned area for scuba-diving! Prices include a seaweed and coral wedding bouquet, diving lessons for inexperienced pairs, the wedding ceremony, a photographer and a videographer.

Cost: Starts at US $3,000 (£1,800) per couple

Contact
Westin St John Resort and Villas
US Virgin Islands
Tel: 0800 808 5020
Web: www.westinresortstjohn.com

Fijian raft and waterfall wedding

For a really exotic and romantic
wedding ceremony, you could opt
for a traditional Fijian ceremony at
the gorgeous Maravu Resort on
Taveuni Island in Fiji. The bride is
brought on a bamboo raft across the
deep blue water, which laps over
purple corals. Once ashore, she and
her partner exchange vows in the
rainforest beside a tropical waterfall.
This amazing deluxe package
includes a Fijian minister, a cake, a
bouquet for the bride, neck
garlands, decorations, registration
and certification fees, choir, dancers,
the Maravu Band Boys, wedding
feast and champagne for two.
Cost: US $1,250 (£750) for the
Deluxe package described above.
Prices start at US $750 (£540).

Turtle Island, Fiji

Contact
Maravu Plantation Resort
Taveuni Island, Fiji
Tel: 00 679 888 0585
E-mail: maravu@is.com.fj
Web: www.maravu.net

Seychelles catamaran cruise

What could be more idyllic than
saying 'I will' aboard a luxury
catamaran and then setting sail
for a 24-hour cruise around the
Seychelles? Couples can exchange
their vows on the *Charming Lady*
catamaran, which has two crew and
all the amenities you could need
including large double bed, hot and
cold water and ceiling fans. The
wedding package also includes
bride's bouquet and flowers,
wedding cake, all meals and
non-alcoholic drinks.
Cost: £975 per couple

Contact
Kuoni
Tel: 01306 747007
Web: www.kuoni.co.uk/weddings

SNOW AND ICE

Lots of brides and grooms opt for
the romantic backdrop of snow and
ice to set their wedding day off
perfectly. Winter wedding
destinations also make great
honeymoons – when you've said 'I
will', a week of skiing, snowboarding
or tobogganing provides the perfect
fun way to round off your once-in-a-
lifetime holiday. Cold weather is
also the perfect excuse for staying
indoors curled up by a roaring fire –
so what are you waiting for?

Canada's Ice Hotel

This is an amazing place: absolutely everything in it is carved from ice, including the famous Absolute Ice Bar and the magnificent chapel where you can exchange your vows. A White Wedding package includes officiant, bottle of champagne, ice cups and one night at the Ice Hotel. There are lots of other options if you've got the money to spare, including a cocktail reception, photographer and arriving at the ceremony on a dog sled. All very James Bond!

Cost: From CA $1,499 (£664)

Contact

Ice Hotel Quebec-Canada Inc.
143 Route Duchesnay, Sainte-Catherine-de-la-Jacques-Cartier, Québec, Canada G0A 3M0
Tel: 00 1 418 875 4522
E-mail: reservations@icehotel-canada.com
Web: www.icehotel-canada.com/en/hotel.htm

Love on an Alaskan glacier

The world-famous Mendenhall and Taku Glaciers in Alaska are fabulous places to exchange vows. Everything will be arranged for you, including either a helicopter trip or guided kayak and hike, to the top of the glacier where the ceremony is performed. The organisers choose a relatively flat location, safe for walking and suitable footwear is provided if desired. An in-house wedding package includes two nights in the honeymoon suite, which has a fireplace, canopy bed, double jacuzzi, romantic CDs and water-view balcony, plus romance basket with fresh flowers, complimentary bubbly, candles, chocolates, bubble bath and balloons! Many more packages are available.

Aspen, Colorado

Cost: From US $950 (£570), plus $600 (£350) to charter the helicopter for bride/groom, officiant and photographer, land on glacier, spend up to 30 minutes, and return.

Contact

Pearsons Pond
4541 Sawa Circle, Juneau, Alaska 99801
Tel: 00 1 907 789 3772
E-mail: book@pearsonspond.com
Web: www.pearsonspond.com

Ski slope nuptials

If you both love winter sports, then what could be more romantic than a ceremony on a ski slope? The mountains surrounding beautiful Lake Tahoe in the US provide the perfect romantic backdrop to your wedding ceremony and you can finish the day off with a sunset cruise on the lake, or take a gamble in the casinos of nearby Nevada. The Ski Slope Ceremony includes bridal bouquet or wrist corsage, groom's buttonhole, bottle of bubbly and administration charges. **Cost:** £320, marriage licence US $60 (£36) extra

Contact

Virgin Holidays
Web: www.virginholidays.co.uk/weddings

THRILLS AND SPILLS

Theme parks offer every sort of thrill and excitement for couples who really love to have fun. And if you want to add a real 'wow' factor to your wedding arrangements, then this is for you.

Walt Disney World Resort

For the ultimate fantasy wedding experience, how about riding to your wedding in Cinderella's coach, having your wedding certificate signed by Minnie and Mickey Mouse, then spending the afternoon whizzing round some of the world's most exciting theme park rides?

The Premium Intimate Package includes a ceremony at the Disney Wedding Pavilion, luxurious accommodation for four nights at a selected Walt Disney World resort, fresh flower bouquet for the bride and buttonhole for the groom, one solo musician for the ceremony and cake cutting reception, two-tier wedding cake with keepsake cake topper and one bottle of Fairy Tale cuvée for the toast. In addition, you will receive a Special Romance Tote Bag and wedding keepsake, a Disney Wedding Certificate signed by Mickey Mouse and Minnie Mouse, a four-hour limousine charter for transportation to and from the wedding ceremony and a reception at your Disney resort. Two Ultimate Park Hopper tickets including unlimited admission to Walt Disney World Theme Parks, Water Parks and Pleasure Island for the length of your package are also included. **Cost:** From US $3,800 (£2,282) per couple

Contact

Walt Disney World Resort
Orlando, Florida
Tel: 00 1 321 939 4610
Web: www.disneyweddings.com

IN THE PICTURE

If you're movie buffs, then the chances are you'll love the chance to get wed where a classic movie was shot. Film locations are also the perfect excuse to dress up and theme the wedding, so if you've always fancied walking down the aisle as Bonnie and Clyde, go for it!

Blue Hawaii

Follow in the footsteps of Elvis and marry at the chapel where he exchanged vows in the cult film *Blue Hawaii*. Not only is this where the King himself tied the knot on celluloid, it's also a wonderfully romantic spot, with the little white church set against a backdrop of

swaying palms and fragrant frangipani. The Casual Blue Hawaii Package includes decorated Hawaiian thatched-roof chapel, bride's bouquet, a ride on the lagoon in a decorated two-man canoe, wedding toast and lots of extras.
Cost: US $1,220 (£733)

Contact
Tropical Dream Wedding
PO Box 422, Lawai, Kaua'I, Hawaii 96765
Tel: 00 1 808 332 5664
E-mail: kkkauai@aloha.net
Web: www.tropicaldreamwedding.com

Pretty Woman
You can head to LA and say 'I will' in the elegant hotel that featured in hit film *Pretty Woman,* starring Richard Gere and Julia Roberts. The Regent Beverly Wilshire is an exclusive Hollywood hotel and the majority of the film was shot in its luxurious top-floor presidential suite. The anteroom, the Petit Trianon, is a popular place to hold a small ceremony, or some guests choose say their vows up the street at a chapel on Rodeo Drive and then have their reception at the hotel. Honeymoon first nights should of course be spent in the Penthouse suite!
Cost: On application

Contact
Regent Beverly Wilshire Hotel
9500 Wilshire Boulevard, Beverly Hills, California 90212, USA
Tel: 00 1 310 275 5200
Web: www.regenthotels.com

Lord of the Rings
Everyone who went to see *Lord of the Rings* and *The Two Towers* fell in love

with the New Zealand scenery. Now an enterprising wedding specialist has come up with a special Lord of the Rings package, allowing you to get hitched at a location straight out of the film. Rockhill offers incredible panoramic views of mountains, valleys, lakes and native bush. The wedding package includes a Mercedes Benz to take you to and from the location, a (non-legal) wedding certificate ready to frame, bouquet and buttonhole, two witnesses as required by New Zealand law, engraved silver goblets, champagne celebration for bride and groom, sparkling wine and finger food, official marriage licence and processing of application. The wedding ceremony can only take place in good weather – recommended months are October to July.
Cost: NZ $3,200 (£1,108)

Contact
New Zealand Dream Wedding
153 Dunbars Road, Christchurch, New Zealand
Tel: 00 64 3 322 4448
E-mail: enquiry@weddingsnewzealand.com
Web: www.weddingsnewzealand.com

Thunderbirds
Thunderbirds fans now have the opportunity to marry and then honeymoon on Tracy Island! Working Title Films chose the idyllic Praslin and North Islands in the Seychelles as the location for the headquarters of the top-secret organisation International Rescue in its recently released blockbuster. For the ultimate Thunderbirds experience, you can tie the knot on

the beach at L'Archipel on Praslin, where much of the film was shot. The package includes a basket of tropical fruit, a bottle of sparkling wine, a bouquet of flowers and one full day's car hire, plus you can have five nights' half-board accommodation at L'Archipel in a deluxe room, then a helicopter transfer to North Island (Tracy Island in the film) for five nights.
Cost: £8,435, to include wedding, accommodation and flights

Contact
Outposts
Tel: 01647 231 007
Fax: 01647 231 008

ANIMAL MAGIC

For some couples getting married is a chance to get back to nature! For a truly memorable and fun wedding day, why not share the occasion with your favourite wildlife, such as adorable dolphins at the Florida Keys or hippos in the African bush.

Dolphin delight, Florida

You could even go the whole hog and marry in a zoo!

Hippo heaven
Weddings at Hippo Hollow near the Kruger National Park in South Africa are pretty special. In fact it's not unusual to see hippos grazing nearby while you're exchanging your vows overlooking the Sabi River. Package includes venue, preparation of documents, wedding ceremony and legal documentation, bridal bouquet and buttonhole plus a bottle of champagne.
Cost: £275

Contact
Virgin Holidays
Tel: 0870 990 8825
www.virginholidays.co.uk/weddings

Dolphin delight
Exchange your vows in the warm waters of Key Largo in Florida, with two dolphins acting as best man and bridesmaid! You'll even get the ring handed over by a dolphin. Wedding Package 2 includes a natural swim session during normal session times for bride and groom and up to four 'swimming guests' and four observers. For an additional cost, you can swim with the dolphins in a private session. Also available for an extra charge are photographs, videos, champagne, flowers and sunset cruises.
Cost: From US $900 (£540) per couple

Contact
Dolphins Plus Inc.
PO Box 2728, Key Largo, Florida 33037, USA
Tel: 00 1 305 451 1993
E-mail: info@dolphinsplus.com

Zoo fest

The Melbourne Zoo is a fairy-tale wedding venue with each function room in a tranquil garden setting. The fact that you're surrounded by the exotic sights and sounds of the animals makes it a unique celebration to remember forever! You can marry in the Japanese Garden, on the Platypus Lawn or under a beautiful Moreton Bay Fig Tree.

Cost: On application

Contact

PO Box 74, Parkville, Victoria 3052, Australia
Tel: 00 61 3 9285 9355
Fax: 00 61 3 9285 9340
E-mail: zvdl@zoo.org.au
Web: www.zoo.org.au

CITY SIGHTS

There are dozens of breathtaking city locations around the world where you can get married. Here are two of the best.

Top of the Empire State Building

It's one of the tallest buildings in the world and the panoramic views of New York are spectacular, so what better place to exchange your vows than overlooking this exciting, vibrant city? An Empire State Building Package includes your entrance fee, an hour on the 102nd-floor observatory, a glass of champagne for each of you and a special New York City gift, and extra guests can be booked in for £10 per person. Packages are available from January to May and September to December, but not at Christmas, New Year, Easter or on 14 February.

Cost: £1,154 per couple

Contact

Kuoni
Tel: 01306 747007
Web: www.kuoni.co.uk/weddings

Sydney Opera House

For a dream day to remember down under, marry at the world-famous Sydney Opera House before staying to enjoy a honeymoon in the cosmopolitan city or flying off to the Great Barrier Reef. Wedding package includes registrar and legal fees, bouquet and buttonhole, transfer to and from the Opera House, wedding music, 12 photographs of the special occasion, sparkling wine toast and cake. Ceremonies can't take place at weekends or on public holidays.

Cost: £1,650

Contact

Hayes and Jarvis
Tel: 0870 333 3838
E-mail: romance@hayesandjarvis.co.uk
Web: www.hayesandjarvis.co.uk

Sydney Opera House, Australia

QUICK REFERENCE CHART

This table can only give you a quick indication of the main features of various locations. In the weather, for example, there are so many variables according to precise location and season so we can only give a rough guide here. For example, you can expect different conditions in Brittany as against the Côte d'Azur in the South of France.
Tropical = Hot all the year round but with the potential for heavy rains.
Sub-tropical = Hot all the year round but more marked seasonal variations.
Mediterranean = Hot, dry summers and warm winters.
Temperate = Warm summers, relatively mild winters and potential for rain, especially in winter.
Continental = Warm to hot summers and cold winters.
Northern = Lots of snow in winter, although summer can be sunny. Look at the main sections for full details.

Country	Region	Holiday style	Travel time	Min age	Weather region	Red-tape factor	Budget (£-£££)	Page
Alaska	USA	country	10	18	Northern	xxx	£££	139
Alberta	Canada	country	10	18	Continental	x	£££	164
Anguilla	Caribbean	sun & sand	9	18	Sub-tropical	xx	£££	71
Antigua/Barbuda	Caribbean	sun & sand	8–9	18	Sub-tropical	xx	££	73
Arizona	USA	country	9	18	Continental	xx	£££	141
Aruba	Caribbean	sun & sand	11	18	Sub-tropical	xx	£££	75
Australia	Antipodes	city/country/sun & sand	21	18	Sub-tropical/Mediterranean	x	£££	132
Austria	Europe	city/country/culture	2	19	Continental	xxx	££	29
Bahamas	Caribbean	sun & sand	9	18	Sub-tropical	xx	£££	77
Bali	Pacific	culture/sun & sand	16	21	Tropical	xx	£££	126
Barbados	Caribbean	sun & sand	9	18	Sub-tropical	x	££	79
Bermuda	Caribbean	sun & sand	7	21	Sub-tropical	xx	£££	81
Botswana	Africa	country	13	21	Sub-tropical	xx	£££	52
Brazil	S America	city/country/culture/sun & sand	13	21	Tropical/sub-tropical	xx	£££	171
British Columbia	Canada	country	9	19	Continental	xx	£££	165
British Virgin Islands	Caribbean	sun & sand	9	21	Sub-tropical	xx	£££	84
California	USA	city/culture/country/sun & sand	11	18	Mediterranean	xx	£££	143
Cayman Islands	Caribbean	sun & sand	11	18	Sub-tropical	xxx	£££	86
Colorado	USA	country	10	18	Continental	xx	£££	145
Cook Islands	Pacific	sun & sand	22	20	Tropical	xx	£££	128
Cuba	Caribbean	sun & sand	10	18	Sub-tropical	x	££	88
Cyprus	Europe	country/culture/sun & sand	4–5	18	Mediterranean	xx	££	31
Dominican Republic	Caribbean	sun & sand	10	18	Sub-tropical	xx	££	90
Fiji	Pacific	sun & sand	22	21	Tropical	xxx	££	90
Florida	USA	city/country/sun & sand	10	18	Sub-tropical	x	££	147

Country	Region	Holiday style	Travel time	Min age	Weather region	Red-tape factor	Budget (£–£££)	Page
France	Europe	city/country/ culture/sun & sand	1–2	18/15	Temperate	xx	£	33
Germany	Europe	city/country/ culture	1–2	18	Temperate/ continental	xxx	££	35
Greece	Europe	country/culture/ sun & sand	3–4	18	Mediterranean	xx	£	37
Grenada	Caribbean	sun & sand	10	21	Sub-tropical	x	£££	92
Hawaii	USA	sun & sand	17	18	Sub-tropical	xx	£££	149
Italy	Europe	city/country/ culture/sun & sand	2–3	18	Mediterranean	xxx	£££	39
Jamaica	Caribbean	sun & sand	10	21	Sub-tropical	x	£££	94
Japan	Far East	city/culture	12	20	Mediterranean	xxx	£	117
Kenya	Africa	country	10	21	Tropical	xx	£££	53
Lapland	Europe	country	3	18	Northern	xx	££	42
Las Vegas	USA	city/country	11	18	Continental	x	£	151
Malaysia	Far East	culture/sun & sand	13	21	Tropical	xxx	£££	120
Malta	Europe	country/culture/ sun & sand	3	18	Mediterranean	xx	££	43
Margarita	Caribbean	sun & sand	10	18	Sub-tropical	x	£££	93
Martinique	Caribbean	sun & sand	10	18	Sub-tropical	x	£££	97
Mauritius	Indian Ocean	country/ sun & sand	12	18	Sub-tropical	xx	£££	63
Mexico	USA	city/country/culture	10	18	Sub-tropical	xx	£££	154
Morocco	Africa	city/country/ sun & sand	3	16	Mediterranean sub-tropical	xxx	£££	56
New York	USA	city/culture	8	18	Temperate	xx	££	157
New Zealand	Antipodes	country	23	20	Temperate	xx	£££	134
Ontario	Canada	country	8	18	Continental	xx	£££	168
Peru	S America	country/culture	14	18	Tropical/ sub-tropical	xx	£££	173
Puerto Rico	Caribbean	sun & sand	8	18	Sub-tropical	xx	£££	98
St Barthelemy	Caribbean	sun & sand	9	18	Sub-tropical	xx	£££	101
St Kitts and St Nevis	Caribbean	sun & sand	9	18	Sub-tropical	xx	£££	103
St Lucia	Caribbean	sun & sand	9	18	Sub-tropical	x	££	105
St Vincent Grenadines	Caribbean	sun & sand	9	18	Sub-tropical	x	£££	107
Seychelles	Indian Ocean	sun & sand	13	18	Sub-tropical	xxx	£££	65
South Africa	Africa	city/country	11	21	Sub-tropical	x	£££	57
Spain	Europe	city/country/ culture/sun & sand	2–3	18	Mediterranean	xxx	£	44
Sri Lanka	Indian Ocean	culture/sun & sand	12	21	Tropical	xx	££	67
Sweden	Europe	country/culture	2	18	Temperate/northern	xx	££	46
Switzerland	Europe	country	2	18	Continental	xxx	££	48
Tanzania Zanzibar	Africa	country	11	18	Tropical	xx	£££	60
Thailand	Far East	city/culture/ sun & sand	12	21	Tropical	xxx	£££	122
Tobago	Caribbean	sun & sand	9	18	Sub-tropical	xx	££	109
Trinidad	Caribbean	sun & sand	9	18	Sub-tropical	xx	££	111
Turks and Caicos	Caribbean	sun & sand	11	21	Sub-tropical	xx	£££	112
US Virgin Islands	Caribbean	sun & sand	10	18	Sub-tropical	xx	£££	114
Washington DC	USA	city/culture	9	18	Temperate	xx	£££	159
Washington State	USA	country	9	18	Temperate	xx	£££	160

USEFUL ADDRESSES

Health
Web: www.fitfortravel.scot.nhs.uk/

Legal
Foreign and Commonwealth Office
Old Admiralty Building, Whitehall,
London SW1A 2LG
Tel: 020 7008 1111
Web: www.fco.gov.uk

Office of National Statistics
General Register Office, Overseas Section,
Snedley Hydro, Trafalgar Road, Southport
PR8 2HH
Tel: 0151 471 4200

Specialist tour operators for weddings abroad
Barefoot Luxury Weddings
Web: www.barefootluxury.com/barefoot-weddings
Specialists in: Bali, Grenada, Kenya,
Mauritius, Seychelles, Sri Lanka, St Lucia,
Thailand

Fireworks over Aspen, Colorado

Cosmos Dream Weddings
Tel: 0870 264 6020
Web: www.cosmos-holidays.co.uk
Specialists in: Cuba, Cyprus, Dominican
Republic, Greece, Italy, Jamaica, Kenya,
Lapland, Malta, Mauritius, Mexico, Sri
Lanka

First Choice
Tel: 0161 742 2262
Web: www.firstchoice.co.uk
Specialists in: Antigua, Austria, Barbados,
Canada, Cuba, Cyprus, Disney, Dominican
Republic, Florida, Greece, Italy, Jamaica,
Kenya, Las Vegas, Malta, Margarita,
Mexico, Sri Lanka

Hayes and Jarvis
Tel: 0870 333 3838
Web: www.hayes-jarvis.com
Specialists in: Antigua, Australia, Bahamas,
Bali, Barbados, Grenada, Grenadines,
Jamaica, Kenya, Las Vegas, Malaysia,
Mauritius, Seychelles, Sri Lanka, St Lucia,
Tobago, Turks and Caicos, Virgin Islands

Kuoni
Tel: 01306 747007
Web: www.kuoni.co.uk/weddings
Specialists in: Antigua, Aruba, Bahamas,
Bali, Barbados, British Virgin Islands,
Cayman Islands, Fiji, Florida, Grenada,
Grenadines, Hawaii, Jamaica, Kenya,
Las Vegas, Mauritius, Malaysia, Mexico,
New York, San Francisco, Seychelles,
Sri Lanka, St Kitts, Thailand, Tobago, Turks
and Caicos, Zanzibar

Olympic Holidays
Tel: 0870 429 2020
Web: www.olympicholidays.co.uk
Specialists in: Cyprus, Dominican Republic,
Greece, Kenya, Sri Lanka

Virgin Holidays
Tel: 0870 990 8825
Web: www.virginholidays.co.uk/weddings
Specialists in: Antigua, Bali, Barbados,
Bahamas, Canada, Cancun, Florida,
Grenada, Grenadines, Hawaii, Jamaica,
Lake Tahoe, Las Vegas, Los Angeles,
Mauritius, Nevis, New England, South
Africa, Sri Lanka, St Lucia, Tobago

Resorts offering free weddings

SuperClubs
Tel: 020 8339 4150
Web: www.superclubs.org

Couples
Tel: 01582 794420
Web: www.couples.com

Rendezvous
Tel: 0870 2202344
Web: www.rendezvous.com.lc

Sandals
Tel: 0800 742 742
Web: www.sandals.co.uk

Photograph acknowledgements

With thanks to all the suppliers of
photographs for the book.
Anguilla Tourist Board 71; Antigua and
Barbuda Department of Tourism 74; Aruba
Tourism Authority 70, 75; Aspen Skiing
Company 14, 146, 179, 186; Australian
Tourist Commission 22; Austrian Tourist
Board 30; Bahamas Tourist Office 78;
Bangkok Cruises 126; Barbados Tourism
Authority 79; Bermuda Tourist Authority
2, 7, 18, 82; Cayman Islands Department
of Tourism 86; Cinque Terre Tourist Board
27; DC Committee to Promote
Washington 159; Dolphin Encounters,
Nassau 182; Dominican Republic Tourist
Office 90; Dumas Safari 59; E. Viaggiatori
175; Expedicao Inca 174; Fiji Visitors
Bureau 178; Four Seasons Hotel 34; Free
Skier 166; Indiana State University 119;

Jamaica Tourist Board 94, 95; Las
Alamandas 154, 155; Leonardo.com 15, 23,
26, 35, 38, 39, 43, 46, 50, 54, 55, 59, 102,
118, 142, 150, 151, 171, 187; Malaysian
Tourism Promotion Board 122, 123; Marc
Van Yper 42; Martinique Promotion
Bureau 98; Mauritius Tourism Promotion
Authority 63; Niagara Falls Convention
and Visitors' Bureau 167; Northern
Territory Tourist Commission 130; NYC &
Co. 158; Ottley's Plantation Inn 103; Palm
Springs Hotel 138, 143; Paphos Finder 31;
Puerto Rico Tourism Company 99;
Seychelles Tourist Board 66; Sri Lanka
Tourist Board 67; St Lucia Tourist Board
106; St Vincent and the Grenadines Tourist
Office 107; Swedish Tourist Board 47;
Tourism Council of the South Pacific 131;
Tourism New South Wales 183; Tourism
New Zealand Image Library 134, 135;
Trinidad and Tobago Tourism Office 110,
111; University of New Hampshire 127;
US Virgin Islands Tourist Board 114, 115;
Walt Disney 147; Washington State
Tourism Division 162.

Blue Oceanic beach, Sri Lanka

INDEX